DOROTHY E ZEMACH
DANIEL BROUDY
CHRIS VALVONA

writing

RESEARCH PAPERS

FROM ESSAY TO RESEARCH PAPER

D1218177

MACMILLAN

Contents

To the Teacher

The increase in availability of information online is both a boon and a challenge to students. From their homes or classrooms they can access a variety of information on a variety of topics. However, not all information is of the same type, or the same quality. Today's student researchers therefore need to know not only how to locate information but how to judge it. As writers, they need to know how to use information to inform their understanding and support their arguments, and (both legally and ethically) how to give appropriate credit to the sources they use.

This new addition to the top level of the *Writing Series* is designed to guide university-level students through their first research paper. Beginning with a review of the essay, students choose a topic appropriate for an academic paper, formulate either an expository or persuasive thesis, research outside sources to support their main points, integrate that research into their own original writing, and format their research paper according to APA guidelines. They conclude their study with an oral presentation of their research, a common follow-up assignment in subject-matter university classrooms as well.

Writing in English is a cultural experience as well as an academic one. Students investigate issues of academic honesty, and learn how to incorporate others' research, ideas, and writing into an original paper of their own in accordance with guidelines from English academic institutions. In addition, students explore issues related to academic research such as judging the reliability of sources, identifying opinion and bias, and organizing and presenting ideas logically and persuasively.

In Units 1-3, students complete a persuasive or expository essay on a topic of their choosing, using process writing to complete two drafts with the help of a thorough peer and self-review process. In Units 4-12, students research the same topic outside of class to add facts and expert opinion to support their points, expanding their essay into a 5+ page research paper, complete with an abstract, in-text citations, and a bibliography. In addition, in Unit 12 students present their research orally to the class through an organized academic presentation.

Throughout the course, students receive support and guidance in organization, language, and academic conventions. They analyze models, and share and discuss their work with their classmates. Both the essay and research paper are developed and written in stages, so students are never overwhelmed, but guided through the process to complete competent work of which they can be proud.

Included in the Student Book are a model essay (brainstorming, edited brainstorming, first draft, peer editing, and a final draft) and a full research paper, with title page, abstract, body, and bibliography. Blank peer evaluation forms are also provided.

To the Student

One of the most challenging types of writing is the research paper. Navigating through the sea of information available online and in libraries and evaluating what is accurate, interesting, and useful is one of the most important skills you can gain not only as a writer but as a student. A further challenge for the writer is using that research to support your own ideas, rather than simply summarizing other people's work and adding your comments. This new addition to the *Writing Series* aims to strengthen your skills in these areas to prepare you for academic work in English.

Throughout this course you will study model writing, your classmate's writing, and your own writing in depth. You will analyze writing in terms of words, sentences, paragraphs, essays, and a short research paper. You will focus on presenting your ideas in a clear, logical way to inform or persuade your reader first in an essay and then in a research paper of your own.

In addition, you will discuss issues related to integrity in writing—originality, honesty, and crediting the work of others. You will have the chance to study some famous cases involving professional writers to see how these issues affect the writing and academic communities.

You should come to your writing class every day with energy and a willingness to work and learn. Your instructor and your classmates have much to share with you, and you have much to share with them. By coming to class prepared, asking and answering questions, taking chances and trying new ways, you will add not only to your own education but to the education of those around you. Remember, the goal of this course is not just to produce an essay, a research paper, and a presentation—but to produce a competent, confident academic writer.

Dorothy E Zemach
Daniel Broudy
Chris Valvona

I *Review of the Essay*

In this unit you will ...

■ consider reasons for writing essays.

■ review the standard parts and format of an essay.

■ review methods of support.

■ review process writing.

I Work in a small group. Discuss these questions.

- What are some reasons university students write essays? (e.g., to demonstrate that they have thought about or learned something)

- What are some common types of essays? (e.g., comparison/contrast)

- Imagine that you have been asked to write a 500-word essay on a topic that is familiar to you.

  - How much time will it take you?

  - What will be the easiest part? The most challenging part?

  - What will you do first? Then what steps will you follow?

2 Read the example student essay. Check unfamiliar vocabulary in a dictionary or with your instructor.

Note: This is the first draft of a student essay, so it is not perfect. You will have the chance to see comments on and improvements to this essay as you work through this course.

Ji-un Kang

English Composition 101

March 15, 2011

Sugar: Friend or Foe?

1   In the developed world, sugar is present in almost all aspects of our diet. The most common sources of natural sugar are sugar cane and the sugar beet. Sugar also occurs naturally in most fruits and some other foods. However, in addition to these natural sugars, there is a huge amount of refined sugar added to the food and drink we consume. Soft drinks, sweets, desserts, fast food, and even salty foods like crisps all contain some form of sugar added to make them taste better. The results of this over-consumption of sugar are worrying. It is linked to obesity, tooth decay, diabetes, and other illnesses and conditions. People should be aware of the amount of sugar in their diets and take steps to reduce it.

2   Raw sugar has been eaten by humans for thousands of years. Sugar is a form of pure energy, high in calories and low in nutrients. Like gasoline refined from raw crude oil, refined sugar has undergone a process to make it easy to store, transport, and consume. Refined sugar fuels the body with instant energy, while also having a pleasant taste. In fact, it is this pleasant taste that is the problem. The appealing taste can make a person want to consume more, even when the body is at rest and has no need of sugar. Over-filling a car with gasoline creates only a minor spill at the local filling station, but over-filling a human with sugar can create much greater problems.

3   One of the greatest dangers of consuming too much refined sugar is obesity. Many college students in Japan and Korea, for example, report that they gain weight during their studies abroad in North America and Western Europe. There could be many reasons for this, but

one primary cause is eating too much sugar. Visitors to these regions are often surprised at both how common sweets are and how sweet the foods are. In fact, when the typical sugar content of the average diet in North America is compared with that of most Asian or Middle Eastern countries, the difference is clear. This corresponds to a similar difference in rates of obesity, particularly among children. Obesity in turn can lead to many other problems, including heart disease and depression.

4   In addition to obesity, refined sugar is responsible for a rise in other modern conditions and illnesses such as diabetes, tooth decay, and gout. By changing our sugar-eating habits, we can reduce the occurrence of these serious ailments.

5   Finally, over-consumption of refined sugar steals nutrients from the body. The body's engine, the metabolism, has great difficulty burning refined sugars, and so it must use some of its own stored nutrients to convert refined sugars into energy. This is why refined sugar has been called a thief.

6   In conclusion, instead of being a useful fuel for the body, refined sugar acts like the body's enemy. Of course, as with all things in life, raw sugar in moderation is both healthy and desirable. However, with the high concentrations of refined sugars in so many common products, eating sugar only in moderation is a big challenge. Everyone needs to face this challenge and recognize how serious it is.

3 **Work with a partner. Answer the questions about the example essay.**

   a. Look at the introduction. Which sentence is the thesis statement? Underline it.

   b. What is the function of the other sentences in the introduction?

   c. How many major points are there in the essay? What are they?

d. Check (✓) the types of support the writer uses.

☐ An example from his personal life

☐ An example from someone else's life

☐ A comparison to a similar situation

☐ Quotations from experts

☐ Statistics or other numerical data

☐ Logical reasoning

☐ Common knowledge

☐ Personal knowledge

e. What does the conclusion do? Check (✓) all that apply.

☐ Summarizes the main ideas

☐ Restates the supporting evidence

☐ Introduces a new argument

☐ Makes a recommendation

☐ Makes a prediction

f. Which arguments did you find the most convincing? Why?

g. Were there any statements that you didn't believe or weren't sure about? How could the writer convince you that they were true?

4 **Complete the description of the steps of the writing process on page 6 with labels from the box.**

Reviewing	Organizing	Drafting
Brainstorming	Publishing	Revising

The Writing Process

Good writing is more than just sitting down at the computer and typing a document. To write effective essays and research papers, strong writers use process writing. This means that they go through a number of different steps that each help shape a final product of quality.

The first step is (1) .... This means gathering ideas. You might make a quick list, design a word map, or just talk with a few other students. At this stage, you want as many ideas as you can find, so write everything down, even if it doesn't seem useful at first. You can edit out ideas that don't work later. The more ideas you have to work with, though, the easier it will be to write your paper.

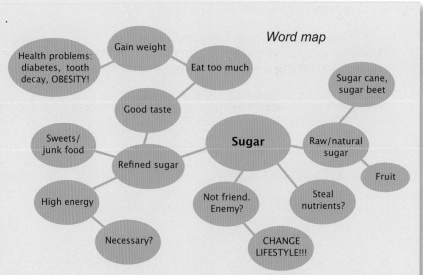

Word map

Outline

I. Introduction
II. First main point
   A. Support
   B. Support
III. Second main point
   A. Support
      a. Example
      b. Example
   B. Support

After you have collected a lot of ideas, the next step is (2) .... them. Cross out ideas that aren't relevant or interesting. Circle or star the ideas you want to use. Number them from the most important to the least important. Then write an outline. If your outline is very detailed, writing your first draft will go quickly and you will stay organized.

Now you are ready for (3) .... , or writing your paper.

Follow your outline as you write so that you remember to include all of your ideas, and in the correct order. Some writers find it easiest to write the introduction and conclusion last; others start at the beginning and write all the way through.

After your paper is written, it's time for (4) .... , or checking. Sometimes you will read your own paper, and sometimes you will exchange papers with a classmate. Make notes about places where you want to add information, where you want to take out any sentences that aren't relevant, and any other changes you'd like to make. Review the original assignment to make sure you have addressed the task and included all necessary parts.

(5) .... , also known as editing, refers to actually making the changes. If you have received comments from another reader, remember that you do not have to accept every recommendation. You are the writer, so the final choice is still yours. However, you want your paper to be clear and complete. Remember to use your computer's spell check program. Ask your instructor about any language or vocabulary issues you can't figure out on your own.

Finally, you are ready for (6) .... For professional writers, this means having the work printed in a newspaper or magazine or posted online; for students, it usually means submitting the work for a grade.

Note: Beginning writers sometimes feel that going through a number of different steps will take more time. However, the opposite is true. Adequate preparation (brainstorming and organizing) means that the drafting stage will go much more smoothly. Reviewing and revising means that you will be presenting your best efforts to your audience, so that your publishing is successful.

Put it together

a Think of a creative process other than writing that involves several steps; for example, cooking a meal, writing a song, decorating a room, planning a vacation.

b Write a short description of what someone would do for each of the steps of the creative process. An example is given below for the process of decorating cookies.

Brainstorming	Organizing	Drafting	Reviewing	Revising	Publishing

First, I brainstorm ideas about how to decorate the cookies. For example, I could use seasonal colors, or make abstract designs, or write my friends' names, or make them look like animals, or color them like my favorite sports team's colors.

Then, I organize the ingredients and tools I need to decorate the cookies: plates, spoons, a knife, colored frosting, nuts, raisins, and sprinkles.

To draft my cookies, I apply the frosting and decorations using a knife, a spoon, and my fingers.

I review my cookies by arranging them on a plate and looking at them. I judge whether they look like I want them to.

I revise my cookies by making a few changes. If any decorations have fallen off, I put new ones on. I add some more nuts or raisins to cookies that are too plain. If there are any cookies that look too ugly, I remove them—by eating them!

Finally, I am ready to publish my cookies. I serve them to my friends at a party. I also serve some tea. Success! All of the cookies are eaten.

c Present your process to a small group or the whole class.

2 Choosing a Topic

In this unit you will ...
- select a topic for your essay and research paper.
- learn the difference between a persuasive and an expository research paper.
- prepare to write the first draft of your essay.

I Work in a small group. Discuss these questions. Take notes, and then share your ideas with the class.

- What issues of modern life are represented by the photos? Are these issues of concern to people in your country? To you personally?

- What important issues have you read about or heard on the news recently? Why are they important?

Choosing a topic

The topic you choose for your essay and research paper will be the focus of your work throughout this course. Therefore, it is important that you choose a topic that is interesting to you, researchable, and possible to write about.

For this class, your topic must:

- **Not be too broad.** Your essay and research paper are both of limited length. You are not writing a book! If you can't focus your research, you will spend your time collecting ideas and information, and wind up with too much to include in your paper. If you are interested in a broad topic, however, it is probably possible to choose just one aspect of it for your paper.

- **Not be too narrow.** You are also asked to present a full discussion of the topic, so it must be possible to develop the topic.

- **Be interesting and important.** If you have some natural passion for your topic, you can probably make it interesting to your readers. You'll know the topic is interesting if you can immediately tell others why the topic is important.

- **Be something that you know about.** You will write your essay from your own knowledge. If you choose a topic such as "climate change" but have no knowledge about it already, you won't know what to say!

- **Be researchable.** You need to be able to find out more about your topic than you already know, and you need to be able to find information easily. Some topics may be too old or too new to be easy to research, or discussed in language that is too technical for you to read in English without further specialized study.

- **Have a point.** That is, there must be a reason to write a paper about it. Are you explaining something your readers don't know? Are you delivering important information? Are you trying to change your readers' attitudes? Do you want your readers to do something? Make sure you can complete the sentence *The purpose of this paper is to* …

2 **Work with a partner. Discuss and evaluate the following weak topics. Why would they be hard to write about? Write changes that would make them stronger topics.**

a. Climate change

....

....

b. Body language

....

....

c. Tuition at my university

....

....

d. Over-population

....

....

e. Teaching foreign languages in elementary schools in my hometown

....

....

f. Vegetarianism

....

....

g. How I became interested in my hobby

....

....

h. The average age of marriage in my country

....

....

i. Income tax

....

....

Brainstorming a topic

3 Brainstorm as many ideas for a topic for your essay as you can, so you will have many choices. Use a separate sheet of paper. Then choose three that interest you and write them here:

a. ....

b. ....

c. ....

4 Work in a small group. Read your topics to your group. Discuss whether the topics:
- are broad/narrow enough
- are interesting and important
- are researchable
- have a point

Then choose one topic that you will write about in your essay and research paper.

My topic: ....

Note: Be honest with your group. If you think a topic is not suitable, say so. You will be helping them in the long run!

Expository or persuasive?

In this course, you will write either an *expository* or a *persuasive* essay and research paper.

• An expository paper explains or describes by presenting facts about a person or subject. The writer might not have an opinion about the topic. *The differences between Cuban, Miami, and Puerto Rican salsa dance styles* is an expository topic.

• A persuasive paper aims to convince the reader of the writer's opinion about a theme or issue. The writer's opinion about the topic should be obvious. *The need for stricter environmental controls for offshore oil drilling* is a persuasive topic.

Note that persuasive papers still contain facts and information. The difference is that a persuasive paper aims to convince the reader to adopt a certain attitude or take a certain action. An expository paper informs, but does not seek to change beliefs or behavior.

5 **Work with a partner. Check (✓) whether the topics below are for an expository or a persuasive essay/research paper.**

	Expository How to do something	Persuasive
a. How Barack Obama became President of the United States	✓	
b. The effects of coffee on the body	✓	
c. Technology's negative effects on social skills		✓
d. Why smartphones will replace computers in ten years		✓
e. Living in the tropics on ten dollars a day	✓	
f. How to survive a Canadian winter	✓	
g. Why public schools need more funding		✓

6 **Work with a partner or group. Discuss whether you think you will write more expository or more persuasive papers in your future courses.**

2

Pre-writing: Brainstorming

7 **Work with a partner. Begin brainstorming in this way:**

- Tell your partner your topic and why it interests you.

- Your partner will comment and ask a few questions about your topic.

- As you answer your partner's questions and explain your interest in your topic, take notes on a separate sheet of paper.

8 **Work alone. Brainstorm for at least 10 minutes about your topic. Use freewriting, listing, or a word map to note your ideas (see page 6 for an example of a wordmap). Remember to keep your brainstorming to turn in with your final paper.**

Note: Examples of freewriting and edited freewriting appear on pages 109 and 110.

Writing a thesis statement

A thesis statement for an essay functions like the topic sentence of a paragraph: It tells the reader the main idea of the essay. However, while a topic sentence of a paragraph is often the first sentence, the thesis statement of an essay (and a research paper) is usually the final sentence of the introduction.

A thesis statement for an expository paper tells the main topic and then usually the major areas that will be discussed:

Sugar, pineapple, and coffee are the major exports of the state of Hawaii.

We know from this that the essay will discuss the effects on Hawaii's economy of sugar, pineapple, and coffee.

A thesis statement for a persuasive paper tells the author's opinion:

Europeans need to consume less refined sugar.

From this, we know that the paper will contain reasons to eat less sugar.

A stronger persuasive thesis statement is one that gives the writer's opinion and also indicates the major areas that will be discussed:

Overconsumption of sugar by Europeans leads to weight gain, disease, and early death.

Now we know specifically which three reasons to eat less sugar will be explored in the paper.

9 **Work with a partner. Look at the improved topics you wrote in Exercise 2. Choose three and write a possible thesis statement for each.**

a. ....

....

b. ....

....

c. ....

....

Writing an essay outline

An outline is your essay's map. The more detailed your outline is, the easier it will be to write your essay.

A simple outline for the example essay in unit 1 looks like this:

I. Introduction

Thesis statement: People should be aware of the amount of sugar in their diets and take steps to reduce it.

II. Background: Information about sugar

III. Over-consumption of sugar causes obesity

IV. Other health conditions

V. Sugar steals nutrients

VI. Conclusion: We should eat less sugar.

It's possible to begin writing your essay once your outline looks like this; that is, once you know your thesis statement and the major areas you will discuss. However, if you can write a more detailed outline, you will have an easier time writing.

10 **Work with a partner. Look back at the essay on pages 3 & 4 and fill in the more detailed outline below.**

I. Introduction: Information about ....

Thesis statement: People should be aware of the amount of sugar in their diets and take steps to reduce it.

II. Background: Information about sugar

Comparison with ....

III. Over consumption of sugar causes obesity

A. Example: ....

B. Obesity leads to ....

IV. Other health conditions

A. ....

B. ....

C. ....

V. Sugar steals nutrients

VI. Conclusion: We should eat less sugar.

Put it together

a Look at your brainstorming again. Cross out any ideas you don't think are necessary for your paper. Add more ideas if you want to.

b Write your thesis statement.

c Write a simple outline first; then add more details to it.

d Write the first draft of your essay. Do not do any research; just write about what you know. Your essay should be about five paragraphs long.

e Complete this checklist about your own essay before you bring it to class.

Does my essay have these things? Check (✓) yes or no.

	yes	no
An introductory paragraph		
A thesis statement at the end of the introductory paragraph		
At least two body paragraphs		
A topic sentence for each body paragraph		
A conclusion		
Correct essay format, including my name, the date, and a title for the essay		
Essay is double-spaced		

f Bring the first draft of your essay, the outline, and any brainstorming that you did on paper to your next class.

3 *Peer Review*

In this unit you will ...
- ▦ learn more about introductions and conclusions.
- ▦ learn to effectively review papers with a classmate.
- ▦ make decisions about revising.
- ▦ write the second draft of your essay.

❙ Work in a group. Discuss these questions.

- Do you like to read your classmates' papers? Why or why not?

- Do you like to have your classmates read your papers? Why or why not?

- Is it valuable to have someone read your paper before your instructor does? Why or why not?

Parts of an introduction

You know that the thesis statement finishes your introduction. What goes before it? Depending on your topic, you have several choices:

- Background information or explanations

- An interesting story or event

- Some surprising information

Additionally, many essays and research papers begin with a hook—a sentence or two to catch the readers' attention. Here are some common hooks:

- A quotation or saying (Find these by searching for "your topic + quotation" with an Internet search engine). Make sure it is actually relevant to your thesis!

- An unusual fact or surprising statistic. This type of hook is more common in a research paper; after all, it is during your research that you would find such information.

- The beginning of a story, if you relate an anecdote in your introduction.

- A question. These are tricky to use effectively—you need to ask a question that will increase your readers' interest and make them want to read your paper to find out the answer.

The information after the hook sets up the thesis statement. It might give some history, especially if you are writing an expository essay, or it might discuss a problem, especially if you are writing a persuasive essay. However, keep specific descriptions and support of your thesis statement for the body of your paper.

2 Look at these hooks for an essay or research paper on sugar. Circle the letter of the three you like best. Write an X by any that you think are not good. Then discuss your choices with a partner.

a. Do you like sugar?

b. "Ecstasy is a glassful of tea and a piece of sugar in the mouth." (Alexander Pushkin)

c. According to the United States Department of Agriculture, the average American consumes between 150 to 170 pounds of sugar a year.

d. How much sugar do you think the average American eats in one day? Half a cup? A full cup? Guess again.

e. I have always loved sweet things.

f. "What are little girls made of? Sugar and spice and everything nice," goes a traditional English nursery rhyme.

g. Sugar is commonly produced from sugar cane and the sugar beet.

h. Question: What do these foods have in common: ketchup, bread, peanut butter, mayonnaise, and salt? Answer: They all contain added sugar.

i. In the developed world, sugar is present in almost all aspects of our diet.

j. Karen W., 23, couldn't understand why she felt tired all the time, or why she had so many headaches.

k. One of the three leading causes of degenerative diseases in the United States may surprise you: It's sugar.

3 Work with a partner. Check (✓) the types of information you think would be appropriate in an introduction to an essay about the need to eat less sugar. Then check the essay on page 3 again to see what the writer chose.

☐ A list of the countries in the world that produce sugar

☐ A description of how sugar causes diabetes

☐ Some statistics about how much sugar is consumed in different parts of the world

☐ Examples of unexpected sources of sugar in our diets

☐ Prices of sugar around the world

☐ A recipe for a dessert that doesn't use sugar

☐ A list of diseases and conditions that will later be shown to be affected by sugar consumption

Parts of a conclusion

A conclusion, first of all, summarizes the main points of your essay. These are what you want your reader to remember most! You may use specific language to signal your conclusion, such as *To sum up* or *In conclusion,* although it isn't necessary. Since your conclusion is always your final paragraph, your reader will know what it is.

A conclusion does not introduce new arguments or important information. These belong in the body of your essay. However, you may logically extend the arguments you made in the body of your essay by making a recommendation or prediction. An academic essay is not a novel; there are no surprise endings. A reader would feel very surprised if you wrote three or four paragraphs about the evils of sugar and then concluded by saying, *However, life is short, so make it pleasant and eat as much sugar as you want!*

Depending on your hook, you might be able to tie your conclusion back to your introduction. For example, a writer who had begun an essay against sugar with the quotation *What are little girls made of? Sugar and spice and everything nice* might write in her conclusion, *A little girl made of sugar wouldn't be "nice"—she'd likely be obese and have bad teeth. Let's make our little girls, and our little boys, of healthy, natural food.*

Conclusions that tie back to introductions, like very clever hooks, are hard to write—not just for students, but for professional writers too. Don't feel bad if you can't write these every time. Often, whether you can write them depends on your topic. However, notice these types of conclusions when you read them in other pieces of writing, and remember that you also can conclude certain essays in this way.

4 **Work with a partner. Read the conclusion on page 4 again, and answer these questions.**

- Did it summarize the main points? If not, which points did it miss?
- Did it add any new main points or support? If so, what?
- Did it make a recommendation or prediction? If so, what?
- Did it tie back to a hook in the introduction?

5 **Work with a partner. Analyze this earlier draft of a conclusion for the sugar essay. Why is it weak?**

> Sugar is very bad for you. Did you know that across the world the consumption of sugar is much more than it was 50 years ago? Also, studies have shown that eating too much sugar can have a damaging effect on your eyesight. This means that everybody should try to eat less sugar. In the future, I will certainly try to cut down on my sugar intake. People should be aware of the amount of sugar in their diets and take steps to reduce it. Thank you for reading.

Peer Review

6 **Read the following text aloud with a partner. Circle the correct verb forms. Then check answers with the whole class.**

A peer is someone who is in the same position as you. In your university class, this means a classmate who a. *has / has not* been assigned the same task that you have. Often in university writing classes, students are asked to exchange papers and comment on their classmates' writing.

If you b. *are / are not* used to working like this, it can seem strange at first. Beginning writers may ask, *How can he judge my paper? He's only a student like I am* or *I don't think I write as well as she does—how can I give her any useful advice?* The truth is, you can help a lot.

Peer review accomplishes two important things:

- It lets you know how well a reader understands what you wrote.
- It lets you see how someone else handled the same assignment.

The first of these is important because writing c. *is / is not* an interview or a conversation. Your writing exists on paper or a computer screen, separate from you, and then someone reads it. Can readers understand what you wrote without any further help from you? Will they notice what you thought was important? Your instructor, of course, is the person who gives you a mark or a grade. But a peer reviewer d. *is / is not* closer to the type of reader you will encounter after you finish your studies—someone pretty much like you, who you don't know, who will read what you write for information, and will not judge your ability and assign you a grade.

The second e. *is / is not* even more important, at least in a learning situation. Here is your chance to study exactly the type of essay or research paper that you are writing yourself. Can you find the thesis statement? Is the support convincing? Do you see what the conclusion is doing? Was this writer able to find an interesting hook? How much background information did he/she choose to include? Were the arguments convincing? Was the paper longer or shorter than yours? You have an example of how someone like you met the same challenge. You f. *may / may not* get some ideas from reading someone else's paper that you can use in the future for yourself.

When you review a classmate's paper, g. *look / don't look* for specific things. Look for the standard sections of an essay or research paper. Make sure you can identify the thesis statement, topic sentences, and methods of support. Note any parts of the writing that you didn't understand—this may mean that the writer was not clear, or it may mean that you had some trouble as a reader. But it h. *is / is not* good information for the writer. Finally, note what the writer did well. It can be difficult to judge your own work, so it is useful—and encouraging—to know what a reader thought was effective.

Most instructors feel that spelling and grammar i. *are / are not* for the instructor to grade, not peer reviewers. Look at content, organization, and ideas. Do not worry about spelling and grammar.

In addition to being specific, be kind. You know that it is difficult to share work, even with someone who is not assigning a grade. Respond from a reader's point of view; that is, say *I didn't understand this argument* instead of *You didn't argue this very clearly.* Give reasons. Just writing *Good conclusion!* j. *tells / doesn't tell* the writer anything unless you say why it is a good conclusion.

7 **Read these sentences from a peer review. Check (✓) the ones that are useful and effective. Then discuss with a partner why the ones you didn't check are not useful or effective.**

☐ Your essay was much better than mine because it was longer.

☐ Your introduction surprised me. I didn't know Americans ate so much sugar!

☐ I think your thesis statement was *Sugar poses a threat to the world's health.* However, it was the first sentence in the introduction and not the last one, so I'm not sure.

☐ Come on. Sugar is not a serious problem. I eat a lot of sugar, and I am healthy.

☐ How come your essay is so short?

☐ You said that sugar causes "a lot of health problems." Can you say what those health problems are? I think that's important information.

☐ I liked the comparison of eating sugar and a car needing fuel. That helped me understand the issue.

☐ I don't know if consuming sugar is the same as a car needing fuel. It's an interesting comparison, but are the two really the same?

☐ Your information about headaches in the conclusion should come earlier, in one of the body paragraphs. It's another health condition, so maybe in paragraph 4.

☐ You will get an A on this essay, I know it.

☐ Nice main points, but your grammar is pretty bad. Please check it.

Responding to a Peer Review

After you and your classmate have reviewed each other's papers, meet in person and discuss each one. If your classmate made any comments that you don't understand, ask for clarification. Answer any questions that were asked.

Then it is time for you to decide how to revise your paper. Remember that suggestions from a peer reviewer are just that: suggestions. They are not orders. If your reviewer says that you have too many supporting points in paragraph 3, you should check paragraph 3. Perhaps you will find that one supporting point isn't really important enough to include. Perhaps you will decide to split paragraph 3 into two paragraphs, or perhaps you will decide that paragraph 3 has a good number of supporting points and you don't want to change it. You are the writer, and it is your choice. Check all of the points your reviewer made, and think about them carefully. Then make your own decision.

In addition to suggestions from your reviewer, it is quite likely that you will find things on your own that you want to change. Perhaps when you wrote your first draft, you didn't have time to think of a clever hook, and now you would like to add one. You might want to add more information somewhere, or change the vocabulary in some sentences.

Mark the changes that you want to make on your essay. Ask for any necessary help with grammar or vocabulary. Then you are ready to write your second draft.

8 Peer Review

  a. Work with a partner. Look at the form on page 21, and discuss the example essay on page 3. Then fill out the form together.

  b. Work with the same partner. Check the sample essay with comments on pages 105 and 106 and then the corrected essay on pages 107 and 108. Discuss these questions:

  - Do you have any of the same comments?

  - Do you agree with the comments the peer reviewer made?

  - How did the writer respond to the comments in the final version?

  c. Exchange your essay with a classmate. Read your classmate's essay carefully. Then fill out the duplicate form on page 102.

Peer review form: essay

Name:
Classmate's name:
Title of classmate's essay:
Date:

1. What is the topic?

2. Is the essay expository or persuasive?

3. Write the thesis statement here:
....
....

4. How many body paragraphs are there?

5. Does the introduction have a hook? .... What other information is in the introduction?

6. Underline the topic sentence in each body paragraph. If you can't find one, note it here:

7. Write the number of each body paragraph and then explain what types of support were used for each paragraph. (Check for a list of types on page 5.)
....
....
....
....
....
....

8. Does the conclusion tie back to the introduction? .... What functions does the conclusion fulfill?
....
....

9. Write a question mark (?) by anything in the essay that you didn't understand. Write a short note to explain if possible.

10. On the essay, draw a star (*) by the two sentences you liked best.

11. Any other comments: ....
....
....
....
....
....
....
....

Put it together

a   Meet with your peer reviewer. Discuss first one essay, and then the other. Remember to take notes on your essay about anything you want to change.

b   Read your essay again. Make notes about anything you would like to add, delete, change, or move.

c   Revise your essay and write the final draft.

d   Proofread your essay by following these steps:

   1)   Run your computer's spell check program. (However, remember that it can't catch correctly spelled words that are used incorrectly, such as *their* for *there*.)

   2)   Read your essay out loud, to someone else or to yourself. This will help you catch missing words.

   3)   Check to see that your paper is formatted correctly (see page 3).

Note: Do not rely on your computer's grammar checker. It will miss actual errors and find "errors" that are actually OK.

e   Beware of electronic storage systems! Make a back-up copy of your work on a flash drive or a second computer, email it to yourself, or use an online back-up system.

f   Print a copy of your essay and submit it to your instructor, together with the peer review about your essay, your first draft, and your brainstorming. Put the oldest work on the bottom and your finished essay on top. Then print out a second copy of your essay for yourself, and bring it to class.

4 Researching

In this unit you will ...
- consider sources of information.
- learn effective online search techniques.
- evaluate the reliability of websites.
- focus your research.

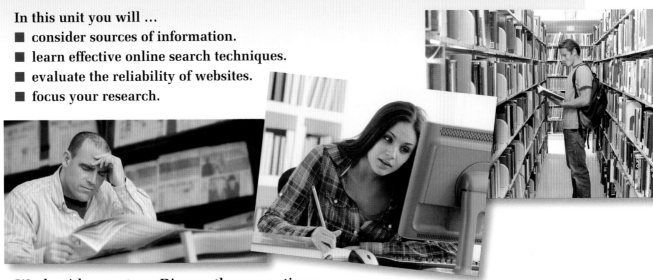

I **Work with a partner. Discuss these questions.**

a. How often do you look for information in these places? What kind of information do you look for? Be as specific as you can.

- a public library
- a school or university library
- online

b. How often do you read these kinds of sources? What kind of information do you find there?

- newspapers
- magazines
- books
- blogs
- official websites

2 **Share your answers to Exercise 1 with another pair. Then, as a group, discuss these questions.**

a. What are some reasons a person might do research in a library instead of online? What are some reasons for researching online instead of in a library?

b. Which of the sources in Exercise 1b would you check for facts? for opinions?

c. Is there any information in newspapers, magazines, or books that cannot be found online? If so, give examples.

d. What are some disadvantages of (some) online sources?

Note: Consider the significant changes that research methods have seen over the past few decades. The principal problem today for researchers is not about finding the relevant material to support your argument, but about sifting through the massive amount of material and accurately weighing which sources can best support your argument. With the information revolution has come an additional problem: deciding which source is the most reliable.

Finding information online

These days, most high school and undergraduate students begin their research online. Sometimes their online searches will lead them to the physical library, but a good place to start is with a general online search.

Popular online search engines include Google http://www.google.com, Yahoo http://www.yahoo.com, and Ask http://www.ask.com. Try your searches with several different search engines and see if you get different results.

Begin by choosing **key words**. These words identify your main topic and also the specific information you are looking for.

For example, imagine that you want to find out the answer to this question:

What percentage of Canada's electricity comes from wind power?

Your key words include *wind, power, Canada,* and *electricity.*

However, if you type those words into a search engine, you will find many more results than you need. Furthermore, the exact answer to your question might not be among the first results.

Use these techniques to narrow your results:

• Use quotation marks to group words together:

"wind power"

Then the results will only show pages where "wind power" occurs together as a group. You will get fewer sites than if you search for **wind** and **power** separately.

• Use the + sign to make sure all words are included:

"wind power" +Canada

• Use the − sign to exclude words you do not want:

"wind power" + Canada −jobs

(notice that you can put a space between the + sign and the next word, but you cannot put a space between the − sign and the next word)

• Use different forms of words if necessary:

"wind power" + Canadian

• Use OR to search for two different word forms at the same time:

"wind power" + Canada + electricity OR electric

• Change the order of your key words:

Canada + "wind power"

• Add more key words:

"wind power" + Canada + 2011 + electricity + percent OR percentage

3 Work with a partner. Imagine that you need to find out the following information. What key words would you use to find it online? Compare your answers with another pair.

a. the name of the current prime minister of Australia

....

b. the dates of the Industrial Revolution in England

....

c. whether the Great Wall of China can be seen from the moon

....

d. at least three causes of the American Civil War

....

e. a recipe for chocolate chip cookies that does not contain butter

....

f. the ten most popular names for baby girls born in the US in 2008

....

g. an image of Rembrandt's painting *The Nightwatchers*

....

h. why Pluto is no longer classified as a planet

....

4 Find the information in Exercise 3 online. Try different search engines. Time each search and write down how long it took you to find the answer.

Deciding what to look for

Searching for a general term such as "wind power" will probably give you too many results to be useful. Before you begin a search, you should have a clear idea of exactly what you are looking for. It is also useful to consider whether you are looking for facts or opinions, so you can evaluate the reliability of the source that you find and the accuracy of the information.

Imagine that your broad research topic is homeschooling in the U.S. You have little background knowledge. You haven't decided yet whether you will argue that parents should or should not be allowed to teach their own children at home; you will probably decide after you find out some information. You know that you will need some **facts** (for example, whether it is currently legal to homeschool children in every state, and how many children are being homeschooled now), **opinions in favor** (for example, parents can teach things that are not taught in schools, such as moral values), and **opinions against** (children won't be able to develop good social skills).

5 Work with a partner. Brainstorm some specific pieces of information you could research about the topic of homeschooling in the U.S.

Facts: ....

....

Opinions in favor of homeschooling: ....

....

Opinions against homeschooling: ....

....

6 Work with the same partner. Choose two facts, two opinions in favor, and two opinions against. Write the key words you would use to search for this information online.

....

....

....

....

7 Work with a partner. Look at the example essay on page 3 again. Discuss what areas the writer could research to find more information for this essay (without changing the thesis statement or organization of the essay). What facts need to be checked? What facts could be added?

Evaluating sources

Of the thousands of Internet sites you will find when you search, how do you know which ones to use? Of course, you want to find the facts that you need and the opinions that you can use to support your arguments. But how do you know if the information is true or important?

Any website that you use should have at least:

- The name of the organization (or person) who created the site, and some basic information about that organization (or person)

- The date the information was posted

- The qualifications of any person whose opinions are cited; an explanation of how the information was gathered

Note: In general, you should not use information that is more than five to seven years old, unless you are writing about a historical topic.

Also look for:

- The purpose of the site (To inform? To persuade? To sell something?)

- Any advertisements on the site (What is being advertised? Why?)

- Any links to other sites (Visit a few of the sites. What are they like?)

- Strong or emotional language that may indicate a bias. Sometimes you will be looking for opinions, but you should be aware of the point of view of the site. In addition, some sites with exaggerated language could actually be ironic or intentionally humorous.

Note: Many instructors do not trust Wikipedia as a reliable source, although some do. Ask your instructor for his or her opinion. Even if your instructor does not trust Wikipedia, it can be a great starting point for finding sources. Look at the references at the bottom.

8 Look at the two web pages on pages 100 and 101 with information about online investing. For each one, complete the information below.

Look at the web page on page 100.

Name of organization: ~~NASSA~~ NASAA .

Purpose/nature of organization: Caution for investors mining for golden oppatunities

信任. ((↓ Date site was most recently updated: Oct. 20, 2010.

Purpose of the site: NASAA is the oldest international org devoted to investor protection.

Mostly fact, or mostly opinion? opinion .

Any ads? _____ If so, what type? _____

Any links? Yes. If so, to what? the NASAA website (.org).

① contact the regulator
② what's New
③ Member login
④ Email updates

Do you think it's a reliable source? Why or why not? _____

_____

_____

Look at the web page on page 101.

Name of organization: Online Investing AI

Purpose/nature of organization: One of the first trading intelligence that uses advanced AI, genetic programming ....

Date site was most recently updated: _____

Purpose of the site: Realize massive trading profits as advanced. artificial intelligence technology trades for you.

Mostly fact, or mostly opinion? fact.

Any ads? _____ If so, what type? _____

Any links? ∨ If so, to what? Email updates.

Do you think it's a reliable source? Why or why not? _____

_____

_____

Documenting your sources

Information online comes and goes. When you find information you think you might want to use, print a hard copy and/or save a copy as a document. Make sure you write down:

- The complete URL where you found the information

- The date that you accessed it

- The title of the article

- The name of the organization and/or author

- The date it was written

Taking notes

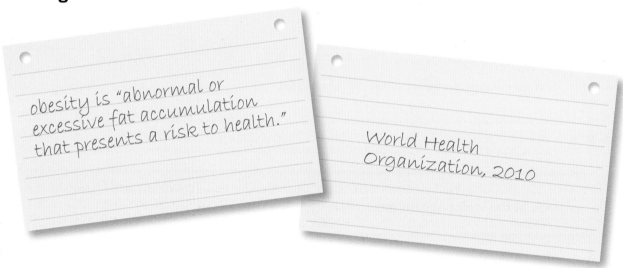

Not all information from one source will be useful for your research paper, of course. In fact, you might use only one or two pieces of information from each source. You also won't use all of the information from your sources in order; that is, you might use a fact from Source A in paragraph 2, then two facts from Source B in paragraph 2, and then a fact from Source C and again from Source A in paragraph 3.

For this reason, it is convenient to put the facts, quotations, and other information that you would like to use in your research paper on notecards.

- Put only one fact or piece of information on each card! This will let you organize your information easily.

- On the front of the card, write the information. It is very important to put quotation marks around it if you copy the sentence (or even part of a sentence) directly.

- On the back of the card, write the source. You don't need to write the full source information on the card, because you have already saved this information on a hard copy or a document. You just need to write enough information that you know which source you got it from.

Put it together

a You are ready to begin your research. Look at the fresh copy of your own essay. Underline facts that should be checked by research. Draw a star (*) in places where you could add supporting information or examples that you hope to find when you research.

If you are having trouble with this step, work with a partner, and discuss together what parts of your essay could be researched.

b Look at the place that you underlined or starred in your essay. Write some key words here that you can use when you research.

....

....

....

....

c Begin researching your topic. Remember that it might take some time to find the information that you need. For your next class, bring:

- One printout of the homepage of one of your sources, so that you can evaluate the source in groups. If some information (organization's name, the date the information was written) is on another page, either print that page too or handwrite it on the first page.

- At least 10 completed notecards with information relevant to your topic.

5 Outlining

In this unit you will ...
- ■ assess your progress with your research.
- ■ learn some important vocabulary for talking about research papers.
- ■ look at common patterns of organization.
- ■ practice different types of outlining techniques.
- ■ write an outline for your research paper.

I **Work in a group. Discuss these questions.**

a. When you organize your ideas, how do you decide which information to write about first? How do you decide the order of the rest of your information?

b. In academic essays and research papers, the most important idea is often discussed last. In newspaper articles, the most important idea is often discussed first. What do you think are some reasons for these differences?

2 **Work with a partner. Tell your partner what your topic and thesis statement are, show your partner the homepage you printed and the notecards you have completed so far, and discuss these questions.**

- What was easy about finding sources for your topic? What was challenging?
- Do you think you have found enough sources, and the right kind of sources? If not, where will you look next?
- What information did you put on your notecards?
- What made you sure the source was reliable?

Vocabulary

Writing a research paper can be a long and complex process, and often involves discussing various stages with your instructor or classmates. For this reason, it is important to be able to speak the same "research paper language."

3 **Match the terms on the left with the definitions on the right. Then work with a partner and take turns explaining the terms in your own words or giving examples.**

a. Argument ——————— **1.** A method of persuasion

b. Body   **2.** A section that directly attacks the opposition

c. Conclusion   **3.** A summary of another source's ideas

d. Counter argument   **4.** Content of the discussion and research

e. Direct quote   **5.** Exact words said by somebody else

f. Introduction   **6.** A section that acknowledges a disagreement with your position

g. Main argument   **7.** A summary that closes the discussion

h. Paraphrase   **8.** An opening that states purpose and goals

i. Response   **9.** A connection from one sentence or idea to another

j. Connector   **10.** The central purpose of your persuasive goal

Writing a detailed outline

An outline is the writer's map of the research paper. It shows the order of the main ideas and the details. Writing a detailed outline before you start drafting your research paper will ensure that your paper will be well-organized, with every piece of information in the right place, and nothing forgotten or left out.

As you remember from Unit 2, an outline for an essay could look like this:

I. Introduction: Thesis statement

II. First main idea
  A. Support
  B. Support

III. Second main idea
  A. Support
  B. Support
  C. Support

IV. Third main idea
  A. Support
  B. Support

V. Conclusion

For a research paper, it is useful to be even more specific. In fact, some writers like to outline almost every sentence! A more detailed outline could look like this:

I.   Introduction
     A. Hook
     B. Background information
     C. Thesis statement

II. First main idea
     A. Support
         1. example
         2. example
     B. Support
         1. reason
         2. reason
            a. example

III. Second main idea
     A. Support
         1. argument
            a. quote from expert
            b. research study
         2. comparison
     B. Support
         1. reason
         2. reason
            a. example
               1. significance of example
            b. example
and so on.

In some traditional classrooms, students were taught never to have an **A** unless there was a **B**, or never to have a **I** unless there was a **2**. However, it makes more sense to write the outline that best fits the information you wish to write about. Make sure your ideas are all relevant and logically organized, and your paper will flow well.

Using a tree outline

The difficulty writers may have with creating a detailed outline is that for a project as large as a research paper, the information is not gathered in order, and so support is not figured out in order, and the writer can get lost or confused.

Here are two ways to prevent this:

1) Write a basic outline on a sheet (or several sheets) of paper, and leave plenty of room to write under each category. As you find more information, write the information in pencil where you think it belongs. This can also easily be done on a word-processor.

2) Consider initially setting up your information in a *tree outline*.

A tree outline resembles pictures you may have seen of family trees. A main (or 'parent') category is placed at the top center of the paper, in a box:

Main Idea

Support or minor ideas then branch out and down from the main idea

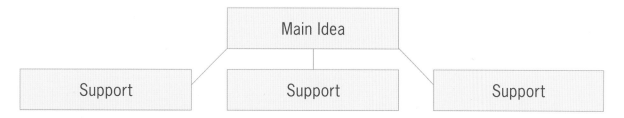

Explanations or examples branch out from the support

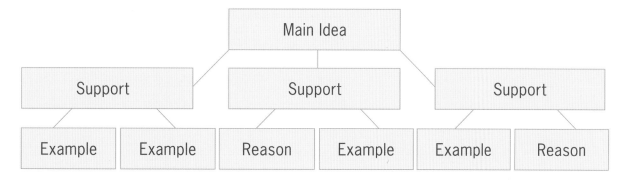

Look at this tree outline for the research paper on page 111. (Note that because this sort of outline runs horizontally, it won't all fit on one page.)

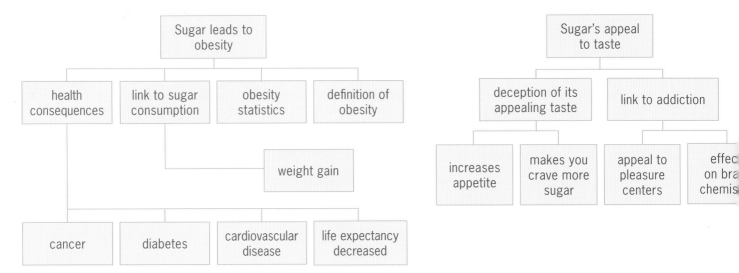

Once you have created a tree outline, it is simple to turn it into a more traditional format. Add the numbers and letters, and then shift the diagram 90 degrees:

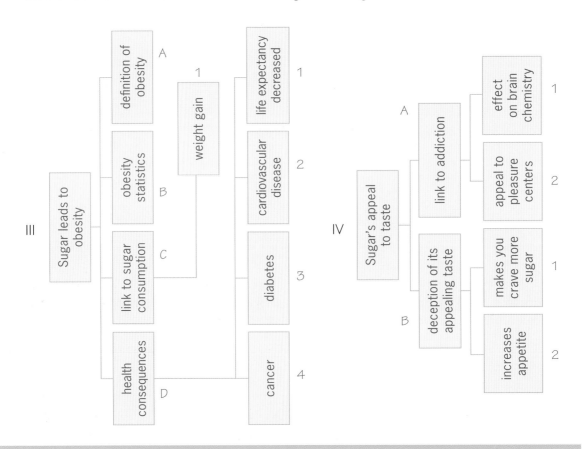

Note: You might want to place some of your information in a different order when you convert your outline. This is fine!

A tree diagram can be as detailed as you like. Whenever one "branch"
splitting it into more branches.

Consider this example from the writer who wants to develop the information
essay into a research paper. In the essay on page 3, the information in the fourth
would look like this:

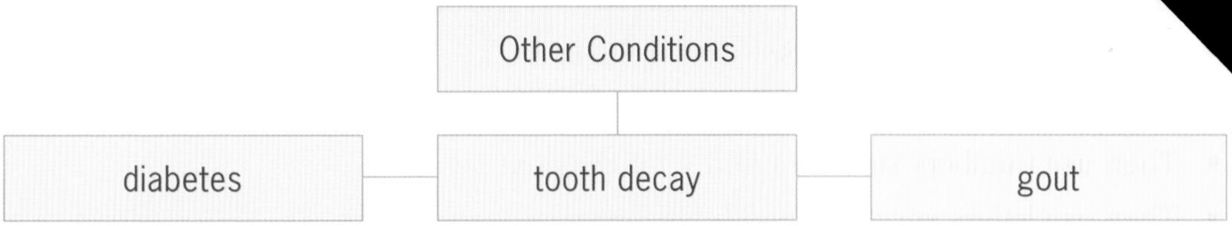

However, to develop this for a research paper, the writer could expand it like this:

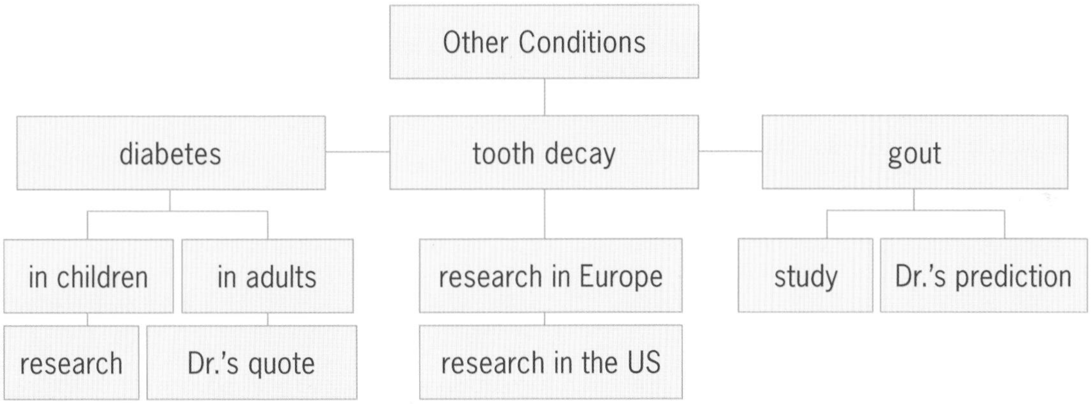

Because this type of outline runs horizontally instead of vertically, many writers find it helpful to write each category on a notecard or slip of paper. Use a wide desk or table to arrange all of your cards. When you are satisfied with your outline, write in the numbers and letters on your cards, and then arrange them or type them up as a traditional outline (which many instructors will ask you to include with your research paper).

If you have never used a tree outline before, try it a few times in this course and see if it works for you. If it doesn't, you can go back to using a traditional outline.

4 Work with a partner. Imagine you are adding a paragraph to a research paper on sugar that covers sources of sugar. Arrange the information in the box below into a tree outline. Be careful—some words belong to broader categories than others! Then compare your tree outline with another pair.

(If possible, write the information on notecards and set up your outline on a desk or table.)

added sources	cakes and pies	fruits	oranges	surprising sources
apples	cookies	ice cream	peanut butter	sweet potatoes
bananas	corn	ketchup	red peppers	table salt
beets	desserts	natural sources	salad dressing	vegetables

from Exercise 4. Can you add one more example to
one more category and a few examples? Compare your

from Exercises 4 and 5. Add numbers and letters to
it to a traditional outline.

Sources of Sugar

for the next level of category

1 and **2** for the next level

and **b** for the specific examples.

5

Once you are ready to write your outline, how do you know which idea will be *Main Idea II*, for example, and which ones will be *Main Ideas III* and *IV*? There are different ways to organize a research paper, and to some extent the organization depends on whether you are writing an expository or a persuasive paper.

Of course, all papers begin with the introduction and end with the conclusion. However, what goes between them depends on what you are trying to convey to the reader.

Expository

In an expository paper, you might present information in chronological order (for example, if you are explaining the history of a city or the development of an idea).

If you are presenting different ideas about your topic, order them from least important to most important. The most important idea is the one your readers should read last, so that they will be sure to remember it.

A typical simple outline could look like one of these:

I. Introduction

II. Past

III. Present

IV. Future

V. Conclusion

I. Introduction

II. Important idea

III. More important idea

IV. Most important idea

V. Conclusion

7 Write a simple outline for these topics. Then compare your
(You may have more than three main ideas.)

- Tourism in my country
- Art in public spaces
- Popular teenage fashions

Persuasive

A persuasive paper can also organize arguments from weak to stro
to more important.

Additionally, however, writers often acknowledge and then refute the counter arguments
against their position. This shows that the writer understands the issue broadly and has already
considered other opinions.

A typical simple outline could look like one of these:

I.   Introduction

II. Important argument

III. More important argument

IV. Most important argument

V.   Conclusion

I.   Introduction

II. Important argument

    A. Support for

    B. More support for

    C. Counter argument

       1. Response

III. More important argument

    A. Support for

    B. Counter argument

       1. Response

       2. Another response

(etc.)

8 Work with a partner. Choose one of the topics below, and write an outline with
counter arguments. Then compare your outline with another pair or present it to
the whole class.

- Video games are/are not harmful for the people who play them
- Electronic communication is/is not damaging people's ability to communicate
- Everyone should/should not adopt a vegetarian diet

...gether

...read your essay. Decide if you want to keep the same organization for your research paper or use a different one.

b   Write a simple outline for your research paper.

c   Make a tree outline of a more detailed outline for your research paper (or, with your instructor's permission, use a traditional outline). Show your tree outline to a partner and explain it.

d   Convert your tree outline into a traditional outline. Write or print out a copy.

e   On your outline …

- Check (✓) the areas where you think you have done enough research and have enough information.
- Draw a star (*) by areas where you need to do more research or think of more support.
- Make a copy of this, and give it to your instructor. Use your own copy to guide your further research.
- Remember to bring your outline and all notecards to each class.

6 Avoiding Plagiarism

In this unit you will ...

- ▨ learn about the issue of plagiarism and academic expectations for original work.
- ▨ learn the importance of crediting sources.
- ▨ understand the issues related to choosing what to quote and what to paraphrase.
- ▨ learn and practice techniques for quoting directly.

I Work with a group. First read the definition of plagiarism from the Macmillan English Dictionary. Then discuss which of the following actions might be considered plagiarism.

---

plagiarism – definition

NOUN / ˈpleɪdʒəˌrɪzəm /

1 [UNCOUNTABLE] the process of taking another person's work, ideas, or words, and using them as if they were your own. Someone who does this is called a plagiarist

Evidence of plagiarism has been found in his latest book.

2 [COUNTABLE] an idea, story, words, or music that you use in your work without explaining that you took them from someone else

---

- Painting a picture of a woman
- Painting a picture of a seated woman with long dark hair
- Copying the painting of the *Mona Lisa* as accurately as you can, as an exercise. You don't show the exercise to anyone.
- Copying the painting of the *Mona Lisa* as accurately as you can, as an exercise. You write "Copy of the *Mona Lisa*, by Leonardo da Vinci," on the back of the exercise.
- Using the image of the *Mona Lisa* in an original collage that includes other elements.
- Painting a picture that looks very similar, but not identical, to the *Mona Lisa*. If asked, you say you thought of the idea yourself.

Academic consequences of plagiarism

Universities (as well as many high schools) in English-speaking countries have set definitions of and consequences for academic plagiarism. Usually these can be found by checking the institution's website.

2 **Work with a partner. Look at the following possible punishments for academic plagiarism. Discuss which of these you think 1) *are* used somewhere, and 2) *should be* used in universities.**

- A warning from the professor
- Need to write the paper again
- A formal apology
- Failure of the paper
- Failure of the course
- Failure of the degree
- A monetary fine
- Suspension from the university
- Expulsion from the university
- Limited career opportunities
- A lawsuit
- Prison

3 **Compare your ideas with another pair. Can you think of other appropriate punishments for student plagiarism? Then check pages 119 and 120 to see which ones are used in universities in different English-speaking countries.**

Defining plagiarism

Even after you study a definition from a dictionary, it can be difficult to define and judge plagiarism. Certainly buying a research paper online and putting your name on it and pretending you wrote it is not honest. However, what if you read a well-known idea from a noted expert, but had thought of the same idea yourself, before you read it? Would it be plagiarism to not mention the expert? Is it plagiarism to use one paragraph from a newspaper or online article? One sentence? A few words?

You can see that plagiarism is not easy to define precisely, even after you have read a dictionary definition. Furthermore, different cultures have different definitions of what constitutes plagiarism in an academic setting.

You are allowed to use the words and ideas of others in your research paper as long as you *give credit* to the original source by saying who the author was and where you found the information, and use quotation marks around phrases and sentences that you have not changed from the original.

If you are writing in English, it is important to give credit in these cases:

- **When you quote someone directly**, even if it is just a special phrase. This gives appropriate credit to the person who originally created those expressions. Like painting or music, writing is considered an art form, and you shouldn't "steal" another person's words any more than you should someone's song. *For direct quotes, you must always use quotation marks.*

- **When you use an idea that you did not know before you did your research**, especially if it is one that an average person would not have known without doing research. Figures and statistics are common types of facts to cite.

- **When you want to offer support for surprising information.** Showing that your information came from a respected source helps your readers believe that what you are saying is true, or at least possible.

You do not need to give credit:

- When you have expressed your own idea in your own way, in your own words.

- For information that is considered "common knowledge," even if you learned it while researching. In many universities, something is considered "common knowledge" if it is easily available from at least five sources.

Imagine that you are writing a paper on the problem of water shortages in the Middle East. You might not have known before you started your research that the capital of Yemen is Sana'a. The capitals of countries are considered common knowledge, though, and you would not need to cite that fact in a research paper. However, if you wanted to include the prediction that the city of Sana'a will probably run out of water by the year 2020, you would have to say where you found that information. Clearly, you did not discover that fact by yourself, so you would have to give credit to the people or organizations that did. In addition, naming your sources lets your readers see who did make that claim, so they can judge whether your sources were reliable (another good reason for critically evaluating every source you use!).

Remember: It is not easy, even for professional writers and professors, to always know what should be cited. If you are not sure, check with your own instructor. It is better to ask 20 questions about 20 sentences than to make one mistake!

4 Work with a partner. Read these sentences taken from the first drafts of university research papers written by students. Discuss which ones you think:

1 are common knowledge, expressed in the student's own words (and therefore are not plagiarized)

2 are written in the student's own words, but contain uncredited ideas or information from another source (and therefore are plagiarized)

3 are direct quotes from another source (and therefore are plagiarized)

Note: It's OK to say "It depends"—but then you must explain what it depends on! (For example, a student's background, or his or her nationality)

a. One time, the United States and Russia was competing with the number of nuclear weapons and it increased till 69,480 in 1986.

....

b. A UFO is defined as an "Unidentified Flying Object."

....

c. To make matters worse, animals will surely eat genetically modified crops.

....

d. Whom did Napster hurt? All those that resisted change, and did not want to make the evolving world part of theirs.

....

e. On September 30, 1999, a radiation leak at the Tokaimura fuel reprocessing plant killed two workers and injured many others.

....

f. For example, women have the right to run for governmental elections in Qatar.

....

g. (The topic is school uniforms) In regard to young children, it is absolutely nonsense to impose a designer's suit and leather shoes on young children, because they do more physical exercise than adults and sweat a lot.

....

h. That Singaporean children don't get enough exposure to sunlight may sound counterintuitive, but in fact the hot and sticky climate makes children more inclined to spend time in air-conditioned environments indoors, and just like in many East Asian countries with more agreeable climates there is also a relative lack of parks and open spaces.

....

5 Discuss your answers with the whole class. While some of the examples can be argued in more than one way, it is important to know which ones would be considered plagiarism by your instructor, at your particular institution.

Quoting and paraphrasing

There are two ways to use words and ideas from other sources in such a way that you are not plagiarizing. These are:

- Quoting: Using the exact words of another person by enclosing them in quotation marks.

  "Ask not what your country can do for you – ask what you can do for your country." (John F. Kennedy)

- Paraphrasing: Saying the same idea in another way.

  John F. Kennedy urged Americans to be more altruistic and less selfish.

Remember: When you paraphrase, you do not need to give credit if the idea is common knowledge, but you do still need to give credit if it isn't.

Both quoting and paraphrasing take skill. All writers, regardless of their age, experience level, or ability in English, work hard to quote and paraphrase effectively.

To work on these skills in class, it is important to have some useful vocabulary for discussing quoting and paraphrasing. Study the definitions below, and then do the exercise.

Author: The organization or person who communicated the original sentence or information.

Quoted text: The actual words taken from another source. Also called a **quotation** or, more informally, a **quote**.

Quotation marks: The punctuation that surrounds the quoted text. American English places periods and commas inside the closing quotation mark; in British English, periods and commas go outside the closing quotation mark. For more detailed information, including what to do with other end punctuation, consult a style guide. Note that while the formatting is slightly different, the ideas of when and what to quote are not.

Signal phrase: A phrase, sentence, or passage that introduces and/or provides some context for the quotation.

Source: Any published or unpublished work where you find the information, such as a website, newspaper, book, podcast, interview etc.

Citation: A referenced source enclosed in parentheses that includes information such as the author's name, the year of publication, or the page or paragraph number.

6 Draw a line from each term to the appropriate part of the following passage.

| author | citation | quotation marks | quoted text | signal phrase | source |

a. ....

b. ....

c. ....

In his *Letter from Birmingham Jail*, Martin Luther King, Jr. wrote that "Injustice anywhere is a threat to justice everywhere" (1963).

d. ....

e. ....

f. ....

Deciding when to quote and when to paraphrase

Sometimes writers prefer to use a lot of direct quotations because it is faster and easier to quote someone directly than to paraphrase the information. However, a good research paper is composed mostly of your own writing (including paraphrases). Quotations can and should be used, but remember that they support your writing; your writing does not support someone else's quotations.

Paraphrasing as a skill will be studied in Unit 7.

7 Work with a partner. Discuss whether you would quote, paraphrase, or not use the information in the situations below. Write Q (quote), P (paraphrase), or X (not use) to note your ideas. Then share your ideas with the whole class.

a. The sentence is a famous saying. ....

b. The sentence contains a lot of technical terms that can't be said another way. ....

c. You only want to use one fact from the sentence, and not the rest of it. ....

d. You don't really understand what the sentence means. ....

e. The sentence is common knowledge. ....

f. The idea in the sentence is extremely well expressed. ....

g. The idea in the sentence is important, but the sentence is long and a bit confusing. ....

Using quotations

It is important to blend quotations in smoothly with your own writing. You can do this with transitions and with *signal phrases* that introduce the quotation. Avoid putting an entire quoted sentence between two original sentences with no words or phrases to link them together; this is known as a *dropped quote*. Your paper will be much more effective with an *integrated quote*, where the reader can clearly see how the quotation supports the point you are trying to make.

A dropped quote:

Volunteering was an important idea to President John F. Kennedy. "Ask not what your country can do for you – ask what you can do for your country" (1961). In 1961, President Kennedy established the Peace Corps, which still sends thousands of Americans to work in developing countries today.

An integrated quote:

Volunteering was important to John F. Kennedy, the President who famously told Americans during his 1961 Inaugural Address to "Ask not what your country can do for you – ask what you can do for your country." One way in which he encouraged Americans to volunteer and to serve was through the creation in 1961 of the Peace Corps, an organization which still sends thousands of Americans to work in developing countries today.

To use quotations effectively, follow these steps:

1. Locate the phrase or sentence you want to quote. In the example below, the desired quote is underlined.

Sugar is not an ideal fuel for the body. Instead, it acts more like the body's enemy. It causes weight gain and obesity, which can lead to many serious illnesses, as well as death. Sugar appears to be responsible for a range of other diseases and conditions such as cancer, diabetes, tooth decay, and gout, and it is actually not at all nutritious for your body. Of course, as with many things in life, <u>raw sugar in moderation is both healthy and desirable.</u> (Kang, 2011)

2. Introduce the quote with a signal phrase.

    *   As Kang says, …

    *   Kang argues that …

    *   In her paper on the dangers of sugar, Kang notes that …

    *   According to Kang, …

    *   …, as Kang explains.

3. Finally, include in parentheses the year that it was written.

    Sugar is not necessarily evil. As Kang says, "… raw sugar in moderation is both healthy and desirable." (2011)

8 Work with a partner. Look at the passages from original sources. Examine the partial excerpts from the model research paper. Choose information from the original to quote. Then compare your choices with another pair.

a. Original:

Refined sugar invades the lymphatic system (disease fighting system). This results in increased white blood cells production and therefore the rebuilding of tissue slows down. The response to strengthening training decreases since the body cannot rebuild itself as effectively. (Ralph Klisiewicz, 2010)

Student research paper:

These negative effects are one reason why refined sugar has been called a thief. Besides stealing, a thief can also destroy things. " ....
.... ," Klisiewicz goes on to say, "... ,
and .... " (2010). Because of these effects, people are more open to other kinds of attacks from disease.

b. Original:

There are, however, disadvantages to the refining process, most notably the stripping away of nutrients and the high concentration of empty calories … The consumption of refined sugar can actually trigger appetite, further increasing your likelihood of overeating. (David Kirschen, 2010)

Student research paper:

So, the highly appealing taste increases the craving for more – even when the human body is at rest and has no need of sugar. As fitness expert David Kirschen notes, the refining process creates certain disadvantages, especially "...
.... ," and this " .... " (2010).

Signal phrases

Here are some phrases you can use to introduce material from outside sources:

To imply agreement	To imply disagreement or doubt	Neutral
Marr <u>argues convincingly that</u> sugar is "a terrible energy source" for the body (2010).	Marr (2010) <u>claims that</u> sugar "is not strongly linked to any health concerns."	<u>According to</u> Marr, "Sugar consumption has risen dramatically in the past decade" (2010).
Marr <u>proves</u> in his 2010 article <u>that</u> sugar is a "terrible energy source" for the human body. However, sugar is actually a "terrible energy source" for the body, <u>as demonstrated by</u> Marr's 2010 study.	In spite of evidence from the medical community, Marr (2010) <u>maintains that</u> sugar is "not strongly linked to any health concerns." Marr <u>asserts that</u> sugar "is not strongly linked to any health concerns" (2010).	Marr (2010) <u>observes that</u> the amount of sugar that people eat has "risen dramatically" in the last ten years. Marr's <u>point is that</u> "sugar consumption has risen dramatically in the last decade" (2010).

As you read and research, notice the signal phrases that other writers use. If you are not sure if they imply agreement or disagreement or are neutral, check a dictionary or ask your instructor.

9 **Work with a partner. Look at the passages from original sources. Then, examine the partial excerpts from the model research paper. Link the quotations to the paper by choosing an appropriate signal phrase. Then compare your choices with another pair.**

a. Original:

Excess bodyweight is the sixth most important risk factor contributing to the overall burden of disease worldwide. 1.1 billion adults and 10% of children are now classified as overweight or obese. Average life expectancy is already diminished; the main adverse consequences are cardiovascular disease, type 2 diabetes, and several cancers. The complex pathological processes reflect environmental and genetic interactions, and individuals from disadvantaged communities seem to have greater risks than more affluent individuals partly because of fetal and postnatal imprinting. (Haslam & James, 2006)

Student research paper:

The health risks associated with obesity are very serious. ....

....

....

....

....

"Average life expectancy is already diminished; the main adverse consequences are cardiovascular disease, type 2 diabetes, and several cancers" (2006). To avoid these negative effects, it is crucial that people do their best to avoid obesity—and that means avoiding sugar.

b. Original:

A new review of the evidence from South Africa confirms that high consumption of added sugars contributes significantly to the incidence of dental caries and obesity. Published in this month's Bulletin of the World Health Organization, the findings cover both rural and urban populations, and add to the growing body of global evidence on the influence of diet on chronic disease. (2003)

Student research paper:

There are other health problems associated with sugar. Sugar is bad for teeth, and is a major cause of tooth decay. ....

....

....

....

....

"high consumption of added sugars contributes significantly to the incidence of dental caries" (2003).

10 Work with a partner. Look at the passages from original sources. Choose the information you think it would be important to quote (you may use more than one quote). Write your own paragraphs with a topic sentence, and link the quote(s) you chose with an appropriate signal phrase. Then share your paragraphs with another pair.

a. Original:

Prospective data suggest that consumption of sugar sweetened soft drinks and fructose is strongly associated with an increased risk of gout in men. Furthermore, fructose rich fruits and fruit juices may also increase the risk. Diet soft drinks were not associated with the risk of gout. (Choi, H. K., & Curhan, G., 2008)

....

....

....

....

....

....

....

....

....

b. Original:

The relationship between sugar added to coffee and other hot beverages ... and the risk of colorectal cancer was investigated using data from a case-control study conducted in Northern Italy on 953 cases of ... confirmed colon cancer, 633 of rectal cancer, and 2845 controls admitted to hospital ... Compared with subjects who reported adding no sugar to their beverages, the ... relative risks (RR) of colon cancer were 1.4 for those adding one spoonful of sugar, 1.6 for those adding 2 spoonful, and 2.0 for those adding 3 or more ... These findings ... would suggest that taste for sugar is a relevant indicator of colorectal cancer risk ... , or a specific influence of even limited amounts of sugar taken outside meals ... (Vecchia, Franceschi, Bidoli, Barbone, & Dolara, 1993)

....

....

....

....

....

....

....

....

....

Put it together

a   Work in pairs. Go through all of your notecards for your research paper. Decide whether the information would work best as a quote or a paraphrase.

b   In class, write two quotes. Make sure each is introduced with a signal phrase and all necessary information. Check with your instructor that you have done it correctly.

c   Check your outline. Where in your paper do you think you could use your quotes? Note the places on your outline in pencil.

d   Choose two more quotes from your notecards to write as homework.

Remember to continue researching and taking notes!

7 The Language of the Research Paper

In this unit you will ...
- ■ learn and practice techniques for paraphrasing.
- ■ look at standard "moves" for performing various functions in a research paper.
- ■ consider common grammatical structures in a research paper.
- ■ review and practice using transitions.

| Work in a group. Discuss these questions.

- In an average week, how many different kinds of sources do you read? Which are formal, and which are informal?

- What are some differences in topics that you see in the different sources?

- What are some differences in the language that you see in the different sources?

2 Work with a partner. Match the texts to the sources. Then share your answers with another pair. Discuss how you were able to figure out the answers.

a. Lady Gaga turns the fashion world upside down with her new 'meat dress' at the Oscars®.	**1.** Mainstream newspaper
b. I understand company policy, sir, but I think that my request for the afternoon off to attend my mother's funeral is not entirely unreasonable.	**2.** Scholarly paper
c. We must all remember that any order for new shipments from Southeast Asia will require a review from the Acquisitions Team.	**3.** Sports magazine
d. Long time no see, Joey! How have you been? When are you finally gonna come down to Brixton for a visit?	**4.** Facebook update
e. Farnsworth is getting ready to light up the barbeque for tonight's blowout with his crazy neighbors.	**5.** Work memo
f. The leaders of the Caspian Sea Alliance concluded a week-long summit to determine which nations would assume the lion's share of funding for the proposed pipeline.	**6.** Email to a friend
g. Beckham's head injury proves to be a massive headache for England's World Cup bid.	**7.** Email to a superior
h. A qualitative approach to data analysis was used as a means of dealing with responses that did not fit into the neat categories of right and wrong.	**8.** Tabloid newspaper

Paraphrasing

Paraphrasing is a challenging but valuable skill. Summarizing someone else's writing effectively shows that you have an accurate understanding of that material. Paraphrasing lets you use information from other sources, but still produce an original work.

Furthermore, if you paraphrase well, you are helping your readers understand the most important points of the issue without letting them be distracted by too many unnecessary details.

Beginning writers often try to paraphrase by using a dictionary or a thesaurus and finding synonyms for the key nouns and verbs. However, this method almost always results in a weak paraphrase, and by some definitions, can still be plagiarism.

The most effective way to paraphrase is to change the syntax of the sentence. Ask yourself, "What does the sentence really mean? What is the main idea? What is another way to say the same thing?"

Look at the examples of weak and strong paraphrases.

Original:

"To be or not to be, that is the question." (William Shakespeare, Hamlet)

Weak:

Being or not being, that is the query, from Hamlet by William Shakespeare.

Shakespeare's Hamlet asks the question to be or not to be.

These are weak paraphrases because they are too close to the original. Furthermore, an instructor who read either of those paraphrases would suspect that the student writer did not actually understand the quotation.

Strong:

Shakespeare's Hamlet questions whether it would be better for him to live or to die.

In the famous speech from Hamlet, Shakespeare shows a man struggling with the difficulties of living, yet unsure if death would bring relief or further problems of a different nature.

Note: A paraphrase can be much shorter or longer than the original.

3 Work with a partner. Evaluate the paraphrases of popular English sayings below. Which are weak? Why? Which are strong? (Note that we have included the 'source' only in the first example, so that you can concentrate on the paraphrasing of the language itself.)

   a. Original: *A bird in the hand is worth two in the bush.* (English saying)

   1. An English saying stresses that it is better to be satisfied with something small that you have than to crave something large that you don't.
   2. A bird that you are holding is more valuable than two birds sitting in a tree, according to an English proverb.
   3. As English speakers say, a bird in captivity is better than many birds that are free.

   b. Original: *An apple a day keeps the doctor away.*

   1. Doctors are afraid of fruit.
   2. Eating good food keeps you healthy.
   3. One of the best ways to stay out of the hospital is simply to eat nutritious food.

   c. Original: *Don't judge a man until you've walked in his boots.*

   1. It's impossible to judge whether people are good or bad without knowing about their life, because you don't understand their motivations.
   2. Until you have walked in their boots, you shouldn't judge people.
   3. Don't evaluate a person until you have worn his or her footwear.

   d. Original: *You can lead a horse to water, but you can't make him drink.*

   1. It's very difficult to force someone to do something he or she doesn't want to do.
   2. Horses don't mind being near water, but they won't drink it.
   3. Even if you explain something to a person, there's no way you can make him or her accept it.

   e. Original: *When in Rome, do as the Romans do.*

   1. Rome has very strange laws, so if you go there, just copy what the locals are doing.
   2. When you go to Rome, do what the Roman people there do.
   3. It's important to respect local customs when you travel.

4 Work with a partner. Paraphrase the popular sayings. Then compare your paraphrases with another pair or the whole class.

   a. Don't put the cart before the horse.
   b. Nothing ventured, nothing gained.
   c. The grass is always greener on the other side of the fence.
   d. Don't judge a book by its cover.
   e. Don't put off till tomorrow what you can do today.

Paraphrasing academic English

Paraphrasing academic English is similar to paraphrasing popular sayings: First, you must understand the idea. Then you can express it in your own words. The most effective paraphrases will be ones that use different syntax. They can be shorter or longer than the original.

To paraphrase effectively, follow these steps:

1. Locate the central point that you want to paraphrase. In the example below, the central point is underlined.

Sugar is not an ideal fuel for the body. Instead, it acts more like the body's enemy. <u>It causes weight gain and obesity, which can lead to many serious illnesses, as well as death</u>. Sugar appears to be responsible for a range of other diseases and conditions such as cancer, diabetes, tooth decay, and gout, and it is actually not at all nutritious for your body. Of course, as with many things in life, raw sugar in moderation is both healthy and desirable. (Kang, 2011)

2. Express the central point in a new way.

   Eating too much sugar is one cause of premature death.

3. Introduce the paraphrase. Here are some useful expressions (note that these can also be used with direct quotes):

   - New research has shown that …

   - It is believed that …

   - Is has been proved that …

   - In his/her study, Kang found that …

   - Kang, in his/her study on … concluded that …

   - In a recent paper on this subject, Kang observes that …

   Recent research has shown that eating too much sugar is one cause of premature death.

4. Finally, include in parentheses the name of the author who wrote the original information and the year that it was written.

   Recent research has shown that eating too much sugar is one cause of premature death (Kang, 2011).

Sometimes, the information you want to use is written with so many technical terms or in such a way that even though you understand it, you simply can't think of another way to say the same idea. In that case, use a direct quotation.

5 Work with a partner. Read the passages about sugar. Use a dictionary if necessary to understand the meaning. Talk about which parts would be important information to paraphrase. Then write your own paraphrase on a separate sheet of paper.

a. The cultivation of sugar cane, a plant probably indigenous in New Guinea, spreads through southeast Asia in prehistoric times. The first mention of its use, crushed for its sweet juice, is in northern India in the 4th century BC. Both sugar and candy derive from Sanskrit words (*sarkara, khanda).* Sugar processed for use in solid form must wait for almost a millennium. The first certain reference to it is in Persia in the 6th century AD.

b. But behaviors that some might refer to as gluttony and sloth are merely consequences of the true cause of the epidemic, Lustig says. Food was just as abundant before obesity's ascendance. The problem is the increase in sugar consumption. Sugar both drives fat storage and makes the brain think it is hungry, setting up a "vicious cycle," according to Lustig.

c. … this report summarizes the results of that analysis, which indicated that most adults with diagnosed diabetes were overweight or obese. During 1999–2002, the prevalence of overweight or obesity was 85.2%, and the prevalence of obesity was 54.8%. Encouraging patients to achieve and maintain a healthy weight should be a priority for all diabetes-care programs.

6 Compare your paraphrase from Exercise 5 with another pair. Discuss similarities and differences. Then check these paragraphs from the student research paper on page 111 to see how the writer paraphrased the information.

a. page 113, paragraph 2

b. page 113/114, paragraph 3

c. page 115, paragraph 1

Academic language: Emphasis

You are familiar with the standard English sentence pattern of

subject + verb (+ object)

The emphasis in a typical sentence like this is on the subject first, then the verb, and finally the object. However, there are some special patterns in English that give an emphasis to different parts of the sentence. These advanced sentence patterns aren't always necessary when writing; however, if you learn to use them, your writing will sound more sophisticated. In addition, you will surely encounter them while reading academic materials.

The passive voice

Voice refers to the relationship of an action to an actor or a receiver. From your perspective as a writer, this relationship helps you clearly see what or who to emphasize. You may shift the emphasis by changing the voice—either to the active or to the passive.

Active:

Researchers at the University of California discovered a new genetic link to diabetes.

Here, the emphasis is on the researchers.

Passive:

A new genetic link to diabetes was discovered by researchers at the University of California.

Here, the emphasis is on "the new genetic link" with the actor (researchers) in a "by phrase." It is even possible to ignore the actor altogether:

A new genetic link to diabetes has been discovered.

Key point: If you want to emphasize the actor, use the active voice. If you want to emphasize the receiver of an action, use the passive.

Some textbooks say the passive voice is too weak or wordy. Some popular grammar websites say the passive creates awkward or vague constructions. Some word-processing software underlines passive sentences, as if to imply that they are incorrect. They are not. In general, active sentences are thought to be "stronger," but the passive is sometimes the most appropriate construction.

Sometimes including an actor in the sentence isn't important. Sometimes an actor isn't even known; a passive sentence such as *Diabetes is considered a serious problem* is more effective than *Some people consider diabetes a serious problem*.

The second sentence, though active, leaves us wondering who "some people" are, when actually the writer wants the reader to focus on "diabetes." Overusing the passive is not good, but neither is avoiding it. You must determine when and where to place the emphasis.

7   **Work with a partner. Read the following sentences. Revise any sentences that would be more effective in the passive voice. Rewrite those using the passive. Decide whether to include the subject with a "by phrase."**

a.   A lot of people are eating more fast food today than ever before.

    ....

b.   The book *Fast Food Nation* exposed the effects of the fast food industry on people in the U.S. and abroad.

    ....

c.   Journalist Eric Schlosser wrote *Fast Food Nation*.

    ....

d.   Schlosser described how unsafe and unhealthy fast food really is.

    ....

e.   A publisher published a version for children called *Chew On This* in 2006.

    ....

f.   In 2006, a bunch of people made a film version of the book, also called *Fast Food Nation*.

    ....

8 Work with a partner. Read the first page of the research paper on page 113. Underline the passive sentences. Discuss why the writer chose to use the passive.

Connectors

Connectors (sometimes referred to as "transitions") are words or phrases that allow you to move smoothly from one point or idea to the next. You probably already use several connectors when you write, especially in compound or complex sentences, and to link one sentence to another.

9 Classify the connectors in the box by writing them into the correct place in the chart.

although	however	in summary	nevertheless	similarly
finally	in addition	likewise	next	therefore
furthermore	in conclusion	moreover	on the other hand	thus

Function of the connectors	examples
To show a sequence of events	
To add more information	
To show a comparison	
To show a contrast	
To signal a conclusion	

10 Look at the connectors in the box in Exercise 9. Which ones do you use regularly? Put a ✓ by them. Which ones do you never use? Put a ✗ by them. Challenge yourself to use these new ones in your research paper!

Note: These are certainly not all of even the most common connectors. As you read in English, make note of new connectors and their function as you come across them.

II **Look at the following extracts from student research papers. Complete the passages with an appropriate transition.**

a. Record companies believe sales have gone down because file sharing provides free music. .... , users insist that file sharing is not the main reason for the sales decline.

b. Royalties from record sales pay the musicians for their hard work. .... , production costs must be paid for, as well as marketing and other expenses.

c. Some musicians feel that file sharing helps them get publicity and make a name. .... , the majority of artists still feel they lose money from file sharing.

d. At first, I copied my friends' music. Then I went online and used file sharing sites to download music. .... I read more about the issue and felt what I was doing was a kind of stealing. .... , I decided to buy songs and albums through iTunes™ and similar services.

e. In the past, before music was available online, consumers had to buy a whole album even if they only wanted one song. .... , the cost of one song or a few songs seemed very high.

Punctuating sentences with connectors

Because there are different types of connectors, there are several patterns for punctuating them. Look at the following examples:

<u>Sentences with coordinating conjunctions</u> (FANBOYS: *for, and, nor, but, or, yet, so*)

Illegal music file sharing has been a problem for both musicians and record companies, **and** *the problem is only increasing.*

<u>Sentences with subordinating conjunctions</u> (*although, because, since, when, as*, etc.)

File sharing grows every year **because** *it is easy to do and relatively risk-free for the sharers.*

Because *it is easy to do and relatively risk-free for the sharers, file sharing increases every year.*

<u>Sentences with adverbial conjunctions</u> (*however, moreover, furthermore*, etc.)

People may believe that sharing songs doesn't hurt anyone. **However,** *when musicians don't earn enough money, they stop making music.*

People may believe that sharing songs doesn't hurt anyone; **however,** *when musicians don't earn enough money, they stop making music.*

12 Add the connectors in parentheses to connect the sentences. Be careful with punctuation. Then compare your sentences with a partner. (Remember that they can be written in more than one way.)

a. (morever) Millions of songs are illegally downloaded each year. Movies are also being pirated.

....

b. (although) Most countries consider pirating music to be a crime. It is very difficult to catch the criminals.

....

c. (yet) Services such as iTunes offer single songs very cheaply. Many people would still rather get their music for free from friends or online.

....

d. (likewise) Some people say that teens who download music should have to pay the fines. Teens who shoplift face legal consequences.

....

e. (furthermore) It's difficult for record companies to monitor individual computers. Some people hide their IP addresses through complicated routers.

....

f. (or) You should pay for your music. You should listen to it on the radio.

....

Put it together

a Work in pairs. Go through all of your notecards for your research paper, but set aside the ones you used for quotations in Unit 5. Choose five that you would like to paraphrase.

b In class, write two paraphrases. Make sure each is introduced with a signal phrase and all necessary information. Check with your instructor that you have done it correctly.

c Write three more paraphrases from your notecards as homework. Indicate next to the paraphrases where in your research paper outline you would like to use the information.

Remember to continue researching and taking notes!

8 *Writing the First Draft*

In this unit you will …
- learn more about thesis statements, and review your own.
- further practice introducing quoted and paraphrased material.
- practice peer reviewing a sample research paper.
- write your first draft.
- investigate the issue of plagiarism more deeply.

| Work with a partner. What differences do you expect to notice when you read or hear about the same subject in these different places?

- A radio interview with one expert / a TV documentary
- a non-fiction book about a period in history / a historical novel set in the same time period
- a personal blog / a newspaper article
- a best-selling book / a movie made from the same book
- a personal essay / a research paper

Assessing the thesis statement

As you research and learn new things about your topic, your discussion of the topic develops from this new knowledge. The ideas you expressed in the essay should grow and deepen. This is a natural part of the process of research and writing.

When you return to your original thesis, you may discover that your original ideas and opinions have changed. This change could be small or significant. Notice the progression of change in the following thesis.

November 16, 2010:
Plastics are dangerous poisons to the natural environment.

January 10, 2011:
Because of the Great Pacific Garbage Patch suffocating sea life, the manufacture and use of plastics should be strictly regulated.

The writer began by making a simple claim in November about the danger of plastics, but after researching their threat, she learned even more about their dangers and felt moved to change her claim in January to a proposal.

If your position has shifted, adjust your thesis to meet this new purpose. This is a perfectly natural result of the process of researching, and if you want to change your thesis (even only slightly) from the one you wrote a few weeks ago, then you should not hesitate to do so.

Thesis types

Thesis statements for research papers are often more complex than ones for shorter essays. Read about these different types of thesis statements.

1. Claim

Even simple observations we make each day allow us to draw conclusions about the people and things we encounter. Paying close attention to what we observe sometimes causes us to respond with a claim about the way things are or the way they should be. Notice the claim about human behavior.

Claim:

Our continued practice of polluting water threatens to destroy all animal life.

The claim remains in the present tense and forces the researcher to use evidence as reasons to show how our polluting threatens life.

2. Proposition

Our research and our observations can also urge us to propose a new path of thinking or acting. This may be because our research has led us to hold very strong beliefs about what needs to be done.

Proposition:

Governments throughout the world should condemn known polluters to prison.

The proposition thesis includes the verb *should*. The proposition calls readers to action.

3. Prediction

Research is a process that allows you to learn new things, to reflect on these things, and to see relationships among new ideas and events, what causes them, and what effects they create. Your research may have led you to an insight that enables you to predict some future effect, upon which you can build an argument. This form of argument is very common.

Prediction:

If we don't restrict the production of plastics, future generations will blame us for the destruction of sea life in the Pacific Ocean.

The prediction thesis includes the verb *will*. This prediction suggests that the researcher has found causal links among plastic production, water pollution, and sea life.

2 **Work with a partner. Read the thesis statements. Write *claim, proposition,* or *prediction* next to each one.**

  a. If current trends continue, we will be faced with a whole generation who only know how to speak through the keyboard. ....

  b. Teenagers should be encouraged to engage in more face-to-face communication. ....

  c. Test-driven language education prevents students from actually learning a language. ....

  d. The danger of not addressing this situation now is that we will be faced with an entire generation who cannot communicate effectively. ....

  e. The rise of social networking has had a damaging effect on human social interaction. ....

  f. Students need to find ways to develop language skills outside of the classroom. ....

  g. Public transport in major cities is not user-friendly for disabled people. ....

  h. If cities do not agree to adopt these new measures, it will send a very damaging message to the disabled community. ....

  i. There ought to be fines for city councils that do not provide suitable transport facilities for disabled people. ....

3 **Work with a partner to examine your thesis statements so far.**

  a. Copy the thesis statement from your essay here:

  ....

  ....

  ....

  b. Copy the thesis statement from your research paper here:

  ....

  ....

  ....

  c. Is it a claim, proposition, or prediction? ....

  d. Do you want to change it? Why or why not? Explain your reasoning to your partner.

  e. Write your thesis again below, with any changes you may have made:

  ....

  ....

  ....

Using source material to support your writing

Remember that all of your research has been to find support to back up your essay. That is different from finding information from several sources, and adding your own comments.

One way to make this clear to your readers is to *frame your source*. Framing your source provides some context that helps your audience understand why you are using certain information. It is not enough to simply put quotation marks around sentences you feel relate to or support your point; as discussed earlier, this sort of "dropped quotation" can be confusing. Creating some context helps connect the quotation to your discussion.

4 **Work with a partner or group. Read the two passages. How are they different? Which one is clearer?**

Passage A

> Of all the non-verbal forms of communication, colour is the most immediate means of communicating messages and meanings (Eiseman, 2000, p. 6). "Colour stimulates and works synergistically with all of the senses, symbolizes abstract concepts and thoughts, expresses fantasy or wish fulfillment, recalls another time or place and produces an aesthetic or emotional response" (Kleynhans, 2007, p. 46).

Passage B

> Of all the non-verbal forms of communication, Leatrice Eiseman notes, colour is the most immediate means of communicating messages and meanings (2000, p. 6). J. H. Kleynhans refers to the subconscious effects of colour and points out that " … colour stimulates and works synergistically with all of the senses, symbolizes abstract concepts and thoughts, expresses fantasy or wish fulfillment, recalls another time or place and produces an aesthetic or emotional response" (2007, p. 46).

5 **Take out all of your notecards from your research, and your outline. On each card, write the number and letter of the place in your outline where your research fits best (e.g., II A 3).**

Note: Quotations and paraphrases are rarely used in conclusions, and are not so common in introductions, although they can appear there. However, research is mainly used to support the main points in the body of your paper.

6 **Work with a partner. "Walk your partner through" your outline; that is, explain what you are going to say about each point. Consider these questions:**

- Can you make your outline more detailed now?

- Do you have enough research, and appropriate information, to support your main points?

Make any additions you wish to your outline.

7 **Work with a partner. Read the research paper on pages 111–118. Then fill out the Peer Review form on pages 64 and 65 together as you discuss your answers. Share your answers with the whole class.**

Peer review form: research paper

Writer's name: ....

Reviewer's name: ....

Title of the research paper: ....

Date: ....

General

1. What is the topic of the paper? ....
2. Underline the thesis statement on the paper.
3. In your own words, what is the thesis? ....
....
4. How many main ideas are there?
....
5. Is the paper persuasive or expository?
....

Introduction

1. Does the introduction begin with a hook? If so, what kind of hook?
....
2. Does the introduction include background information? If so, about what?
....
3. Is the thesis statement the final sentence of the introduction? ....

Body

1. How many body paragraphs are there? ....
2. Underline the topic sentence in each body paragraph.
3. For each body paragraph, write the types of support that appear (e.g., statistics, results of a study, expert testimony, personal experience, logical reasoning, etc).
....
....
....
....
....
....
....
4. How are the body paragraphs arranged? (e.g., chronologically; least important to most important idea; no particular order)
....
....

5. Which piece of research do you find the most convincing?

....

....

....

6. Is there any research that you think does not support the author's point? If so, explain here:

....

....

....

7. Are there any points that you feel need more support? If so, explain here:

....

....

....

Conclusion

1. Does the conclusion tie back to the introduction? If so, how?

....

....

2. Does the conclusion summarize the main points?

....

3. Are any new points raised in the conclusion? If so, what?

....

....

....

4. What else does the conclusion do? (eg, make a prediction or recommendation)

....

General impressions

1. What are two things you learned from reading this paper?

....

....

....

2. Draw a star (*) by your two favorite sentences in the paper.

Put it together

Normally, this assignment comes at the end of a unit. However, writing the first draft is a long task. For this reason, we have moved it to the middle of this unit, so that you will have more time to complete it. While you are writing your first draft at home, you will be discussing issues in class that are related to writing.

a **Assemble all of your materials: Your essay, your outline, your notecards, and your textbook.**

b **Do not worry at this stage about a title page, an abstract, or a final bibliography. Those will be added later.**

c **Start writing!**
  - Some writers find it helpful to paste their outline into a document, and then add to each section (erasing the outline part after they have finished a section). This way, they can be sure that they will follow the organization they chose.

  - Some writers find it easier to write the introduction last, or just before they write the conclusion. You may write your sections in any order, but refer to your outline frequently to make sure you stay organized.

d **Print two hard copies of your research paper when you are finished. Bring one to class to work on, and keep the other in a safe place. Additionally, you should keep electronic back-ups of your work on a flash drive, emailed to yourself, or on an online server.**

8 **Work in a group. Discuss these issues.**

   a. You have already discussed the issue of academic plagiarism in academic papers, in Unit 6. What, if anything, do you think would constitute plagiarism in:

- popular music

- popular fiction

- a newspaper

- a personal blog

- popular non-fiction

   b. If someone is guilty of plagiarism in one of the above cases, what (if anything) should the punishment be?

   c. Do you know of any famous cases of plagiarism? If so, explain them to your group.

Now read the passage below.

A Case of Plagiarism?

Stephen Ambrose (1936–2002) was a famous American historian, professor and author. He wrote biographies of American presidents and also historical accounts of the American civil war, World War II, and other major periods of American history. He was the military advisor for the World War II movie *Saving Private Ryan*, and won dozens of literary and civil awards for his work, including an Emmy for his role as a producer for the television miniseries Band of Brothers.

In 2002, Ambrose was accused of plagiarism by the American magazine *The Weekly Standard*. It claimed that Ambrose's popular book on World War II aviation, *The Wild Blue*, had used passages from an earlier work by Thomas Childers called *Wings of Morning*.

The passages that Ambrose used were footnoted; that is, he did credit Childers. However, he didn't use quotation marks around passages that many people feel were direct quotes. In his own defense, Ambrose explained in an interview with the New York Times in 2002 that he is not an academic writing a Ph.D. dissertation, but rather a storyteller, and he concentrates on the story itself, not the sources. He pointed out that he does put in footnotes, and regretted in that case not including the quotation marks, but that there was no intention to steal anything, since the original source was credited.

Both Mr. Ambrose and his publisher issued an apology to Professor Childers, and later editions of *The Wild Blue* did include the quotation marks. However, the damage to Ambrose's reputation was probably permanent, particularly as other books of his were challenged for similar issues.

9 Work in a group. Read the original passage from *Wings of Morning* and Ambrose's passage from *The Wild Blue*. Then discuss the questions.

Up, up, up, groping through the clouds for what seemed like an eternity. (…) No amount of practice could have prepared them for what they encountered. B-24's, glittering like mica, were popping up out of the clouds all over the sky. Childers, T. (1995). Wings of morning: the story of the last American bomber shot down over Germany in World War II. Reading, MA: Perseus Books, p. 83.	Up, up, up he went, until he got above the clouds. No amount of practice could have prepared the pilot and crew for what they encountered—B-24's, glittering like mica, were popping up out of the clouds over here, over there, everywhere. The Wild Blue: The Men and Boys Who Flew the B-24s over Germany, Stephen Ambrose, New York: Simon & Schuster, 2001, p. 164.

a. Do you think what Ambrose did was plagiarism? Why or why not? If you say yes, explain exactly which words / phrases / sentences / information constitute plagiarism.

b. If it was plagiarism, why do you think he did it? How did it happen?

c. What should Mr. Ambrose have done about the issue?

d. Could such a case happen in your country? What would the reaction be? How would it be handled?

10 Read the following comment. Discuss it with the class. Do you agree or disagree, and why?

Even if you use quotation marks for all of the sentences you use from other sources, it's not really "good writing" unless most of it is your own. Good writing is not simply collecting the best sentences from other people and putting them together; good writing must include originality as well.

11 Work in pairs or small groups. Write your own paraphrase of the passage from *Wings of Morning*. Then write your paraphrases on the board and discuss these questions with the whole class.

- How were the paraphrases similar? How were they different?
- What was challenging about paraphrasing this passage?
- How long did it take to write an acceptable paraphrase?

12 Work with a partner. Share and discuss your paraphrases in your research paper and the original passages they came from. Do you agree that the paraphrases are adequate? Make any desired changes now.

9 In-Text Citations

In this unit you will …

■ learn about correct formatting for APA-style in-text citations.

■ practice further deciding whether to paraphrase or quote.

■ practice paraphrasing and quoting, using correct in-text citations.

■ conduct a peer review of a classmate's research paper.

I **Work with a partner or group. Discuss these questions.**

• When you read published research, why is it important to know where the authors found their information?

• As a reader, when you are reading information in a report that came from somewhere else, how and where do you like to be told about that—in the body of the paper? At the bottom of the page? At the end of the paper? Somewhere else?

• Have you ever looked up a source that was mentioned somewhere else, such as in an online report or blog, or in a book? If so, describe the circumstances. What made it possible for you to find that original source?

2 **Work with a partner. Exchange research papers. Complete the peer review form on page 103. When you have both finished, meet with your partner and discuss the peer review forms one at a time.**

Making revision decisions

A peer review gives you one reader's impressions of your research paper. Based on this feedback, what you noticed from reading someone else's paper, and your own ideas, you may wish to make changes in your paper. Mark these changes on your hard copy so you won't forget them.

Remember that you are not obligated to change something that your reviewer did not like or understand, as long as you have checked it carefully and are convinced that your paper is the way you want it. However, if your reviewer, for example, had difficulty finding your topic sentences, then that should be a signal to you to check your topic sentences. Are they really clear? Are they located in the correct place?

A short guide to APA style

APA stands for the *American Psychological Association*.

The *Publication Manual of the American Psychological Association* is a collection of rules for academic writing. When you write an academic paper, you can refer to the manual to find out how to format your paper, credit your sources, and address issues of style, grammar, and punctuation.

3 **Work with a partner. In each group of examples, check (✓) the format that you think is correct.**

a. My family play soccer. ....

My family plays soccer. ....

b. 5 people came to the party. ....

Five people came to the party. ....

c. *Alice in Wonderland* ....

Alice in wonderland ....

Alice In Wonderland ....

d. He didn't do it. ....

He did not do it. ....

e. Plagiarism is one of the most important issues that I learned about in this course. ....

Plagiarism is one of the most important issues which I learned about in this course. ....

f. Geothermal, wind, and solar power are popular types of alternative energy sources. ....

Geothermal, wind and solar power are popular types of alternative energy sources. ....

Actually, none of these sentences is totally wrong. However, the *Publication Manual* clearly states that in each case one sentence is more appropriate than the other. The *Publication Manual* presents the rules needed for writing an academic paper, such as the research paper you are working on. For more details go to the APA website and view the tutorial at http://www.apastyle.org/learn/tutorials/basics-tutorial.aspx

The purpose of following APA style

Following a standardized set of style guidelines helps to avoid confusion and to make your writing as clear as possible.

APA is not the only set of style guidelines to follow. There are in fact many guides, including **The Oxford Guide to Style** and **The Chicago Manual of Style**, as well as specific guides for different branches of science and other fields. One style guide is not better than any other. The important thing is to follow the style guide for the type of writing that you are doing. We have chosen APA style for this textbook because it is commonly used in a variety of undergraduate disciplines in English-language universities.

Because in your life as a student, a researcher, and a writer, you might need to use different style guides at different times, it is not recommended that you try to memorize the formatting or rules from any one guide. Instead, become accustomed to following a guide like a rule book. You can apply the same good habits to any guide.

This textbook cannot possibly cover all of the material covered in an APA style guide. You can find some information online, but if you will be writing research papers in the future that use this style, we strongly recommend purchasing your own copy of an APA style guide.

APA citation style

Sources are credited in two places: In the body of your paper, and on a separate page at the end of your paper. In the main body of your paper, write the name of the author who wrote the information you are citing (or the name of the publication or organization if there is no named author), and the year it was written. A more detailed reference list at the end of the paper gives the reader all of the information needed to locate the source.

In-text citations

A citation is a very important sign that tells readers two things simultaneously: you are both an honest and a careful researcher. If you do not clearly alert readers to the information you are borrowing with proper citations, you may be perceived as either dishonest or careless. Much like your developing various other physical and mental abilities, your researching skills also develop through good practice. Using citations properly is no exception to excellent researching practice. Note how simple citing a source can be.

Here are some basic rules:

Quotations

1. If the quotation is short (fewer than 40 words), include it directly in the text. Use double quotation marks [" … "]. Where possible, include the page number after the quotation.

Examples:

Thrasher (2006) stated that there was, "no chance a new parking lot could be built within the existing grounds" (p. 239), although this was before the full extent of the problem had become known.

Naomi Klein observed that the "pillage of the incredible natural resources of the Americas that generated the excess capital made the Industrial Revolution possible" (2009).

2. If there are more than 40 words, put the quote in a freestanding block and indent the block approximately 1.3 cm from the left margin. Single-space the indented block.

Example:

Park (2001) claimed the following:

> *If the rats were fed purely on cheeseburgers for the duration of the experiment, the resultant lack of activity and lack of desire to exercise increased their weight gain by three times the control group. This conclusively shows that it is the extra cheese consumed on a daily basis, and not the burger itself as was previously thought, that is responsible. (p. 1280)*

Note: You can see that there is a difference between the short quote and the long quote regarding where to put periods. Find the difference now and check with a partner that you understand that difference.

Paraphrases

Write the surname of the author and the year in parentheses at the relevant point in the paraphrase. Note that if you write the author's name in the main body, you do not need to repeat it in parentheses. You can even mention more than one source for the same point.

Examples:

Hamagawa (2009) found that drinking coffee …

In a study of coffee (Hamagawa, 2009), it was concluded that …

Naomi Klein has recently argued that the Industrial Revolution could not have begun without the rape and pillage of America's vast natural resources (2009).

Investigations into the negative effects of sleep deprivation (Sueyoshi, 2008; Suh, 2010) conclusively prove that …

4 Work with a partner. Look at the research paper on pages 111–118. How many quotations are there? How many paraphrases are there? Circle any signal phrases that you find.

Extended practice with in-text citations

5 Read the following article about the accuracy of science in popular movies. Check any unfamiliar vocabulary in a dictionary. You will use this article for the next two exercises.

Discover.com

Science and movies: My new essay in *Nature*

by Carl Zimmer

November 3, 2010

It is odd that science and films have such a complicated relationship, given that films were born out of science. The invention of photography in the nineteenth century made it possible to capture a series of images and use them to create an illusion of movement. With the development of faster cameras, movies began to seduce the world. Each technical advance has brought change to the cinema, although not every change has resulted in artistic progress — witness Smell-O-Vision and Piranha 3D, for example.

For all that science and technology have delivered to Hollywood, scientists have received little back. Researchers portrayed in films bear scant resemblance to those in real labs. Some on-screen scientists are villains that must be destroyed by common-sense heroes. Others threaten nature with Promethean recklessness. Yet others are mavericks who find cures for cancer single-handedly in jungle tree-houses. And movies often distort science itself. Tornadoes, volcanoes, spaceships, viruses: all obey the laws of Hollywood, not the laws of Newton or Darwin.

Scientists have gnashed their popcorn buckets, wishing for something better. In 2008, the US National Academy of Sciences set up the Science and Entertainment Exchange to bring scientists and Hollywood film-makers together for fruitful exchanges of ideas. Gambis's film festival serves a similar mission: its website announces that it "encourages a greater collaboration between scientists who dedicate their lives to studying the world we live in and film-makers who have the power to interpret and expose this knowledge, ultimately making science accessible and stimulating to a broader audience."

I'm not convinced such collaborations will achieve this goal often, or even whether they should. Exhibit A: Harrison Ford. Earlier this year, he played a biochemist searching for a cure for a genetic disorder in *Extraordinary Measures*, a fairly accurate story inspired by a book by reporter Geeta Anand. In 2008, Ford also played a scientist in *Indiana Jones and the Kingdom of the Crystal Skull*, a fairly accurate account of a comic-book fever dream. *Extraordinary Measures* earned a meagre US$12 million, whereas *Indiana Jones and the Kingdom of the Crystal Skull* earned $317 million. Hollywood is a place of business, not charity, and the marketplace speaks clearly: people want their scientists with bullwhips, not pipettes.

Even if Hollywood directors dedicated themselves to achingly realistic biopics about Peter Medawar or Henri Poincaré, that might not be a good thing. Films should not be propaganda, bludgeoning us with messages about how valuable certain things or people are. At their best, films embody the conflicts in our societies, and give form to our inner lives in all their ragged glory. They can use real aspects of the world as their raw material, but holding them drearily to account is a mistake. *Citizen Kane* is about a newspaper editor; it would not have been a masterpiece if Orson Welles had kept asking himself "Does this make journalism accessible to a broader audience?"

6 **Work with a partner. Use quotes from the following excerpts in an original sentence of your own. Follow the example. Use an in-text citation.**

Example:

With the development of faster cameras, movies began to seduce the world.

1) Blogger Carl Zimmer notes that the introduction of faster movie cameras marked the point at which movies "began to seduce the world" (2010).

2) "With the development of faster cameras, movies began to seduce the world," Carl Zimmer explained in his blog of November 2, 2010.

a. Yet others are mavericks who find cures for cancer single-handedly in jungle tree-houses.

b. Films should not be propaganda, bludgeoning us with messages about how valuable certain things or people are.

c. At their best, films embody the conflicts in our societies, and give form to our inner lives in all their ragged glory.

7 **Work with a partner. Paraphrase the following excerpts. You may add a comment of your own if you like. Follow the example. Decide whether you need to add an in-text citation (determine whether the information is common knowledge, or whether you learned it from reading the article), and add one where necessary.**

Example:

Each technical advance has brought change to the cinema, although not every change has resulted in artistic progress—witness Smell-O-Vision and Piranha 3D, for example.

1) Not every scientific advance in the field of movie making has been an improvement; blogger Carl Zimmer gives the examples of Smell-O-Vision and Piranha 3D (2010).

2) Smell-O-Vision and Piranha 3D are two examples of technological advances that didn't actually help the filmmaking industry (Zimmer, 2010), which reminds us that not every new invention is something that will be beneficial or that will last.

a. Researchers portrayed in films bear scant resemblance to those in real labs.

b. Tornadoes, volcanoes, spaceships, viruses: all obey the laws of Hollywood, not the laws of Newton or Darwin.

c. In 2008, the US National Academy of Sciences set up the Science and Entertainment Exchange to bring scientists and Hollywood film-makers together for fruitful exchanges of ideas.

d. *Extraordinary Measures* earned a meagre US$12 million, whereas *Indiana Jones and the Kingdom of the Crystal Skull* earned $317 million.

e. Hollywood is a place of business, not charity, and the marketplace speaks clearly: people want their scientists with bullwhips, not pipettes.

Put it together

a Look over the peer review you received of your first draft. Make sure you understand any comments and questions your reviewer made. Then make notes for yourself about any parts of your paper you want to change based on this review.

b Read your paper again to yourself. You may find ideas, explanations, or comments that you want to add; sentences that you wish to delete; or sentences or ideas you would like to put in another place.

c Locate all of the places where you used quotations or paraphrases. Add the in-text citations. If you have questions about formatting or punctuation, check the examples in this unit, check online, or ask your instructor for help.

d You will complete a second draft of your paper after Unit 10. However, any time that you wish to make a change, it is perfectly OK to do so. As with previous drafts, remember to save a copy of your paper in more than one place. You may also wish to save copies of your first draft, in case you decide to undo a change.

10 Academic Language

In this unit you will ...

- consider appropriate style and tone for academic work.
- learn how to make your points stronger and more precise.
- learn about avoiding phrasal verbs and idioms.
- consider qualifying your thesis statement.
- use hedging language to make claims and assertions more believable and accurate.
- write a second draft of your paper.

I   **Work with a partner. Look at the picture. Discuss with your partner who the people are, and where you think they might be. Then read the dialogue. Do you think it is appropriate? Why or why not?**

Woman:	So, is skateboarding now permitted on campus?
Boy:	Dunno. Maybe.
Woman:	Would it not be a good idea to check?
Boy:	Everyone else is doing it, must be OK.
Woman:	Doing what? Ignoring the rules, or skateboarding?
Boy:	What? Are you the skateboard police?

Just as there are appropriate and inappropriate ways to talk with people depending on the situation, so are there appropriate words and expressions to use when writing an academic piece of work. In this unit we will look at some of those more appropriate academic styles.

Academic style and tone

Academic style, in addition to being formal, includes being precise. The more clearly your vocabulary expresses what you mean, the better the chance your reader will get your points.

For example, a sentence such as this is vague:

Sebastian Jimenez is a good soccer player.

What does "good" mean? Is he successful? Does he train hard? Is she well-known? Is he a good team player?

Beginning writers sometimes try to "strengthen" their writing by simply making vague words stronger. However, the following sentences are no clearer:

Sebastian Jimenez is an excellent soccer player.

Sebastian Jimenez is an amazing soccer player.

We still don't really know what qualities he has or displays that make him remarkable.

The following sentences are more precise:

Sebastian Jimenez has remarkable endurance and is a quick sprinter.

Sebastian Jimenez has good "field vision": At any time, he knows where his teammates are and where his opponents are.

It is natural to have a larger reading vocabulary than an active writing vocabulary. As you edit your first draft, though, look for places where your language is weak or imprecise. You can strengthen these sentences by substituting stronger, more descriptive words, or by adding explanations and examples.

2 **Classify the words in the box by writing them into the correct column. Add two more words to each column. Then discuss with a partner which words can be used to describe these things:**

- objects
- ideas or plans
- people

clever	impractical	obsolete	unfounded
efficient	innovative	overwhelming	unpopular
faulty	misguided	stubborn	visionary

positive	negative

3 **Work with a partner. Rewrite the following sentences to make them stronger. You can change words or phrases; however, keep the overall meaning the same. Then share your new sentences with another pair.**

   a. Overpopulation is a real problem.

   b. Convincing people in some cultures to have fewer children is difficult.

   c. Many people like large families.

   d. They think having a lot of children is good.

   e. However, living in a world without enough food or energy for everyone would be bad.

   f. Education is important.

   g. Understanding and respecting people's cultures is important, too.

Phrasal verbs and idioms

Academic styles of writing are usually marked by precision and concision. Casual conversation, though, isn't usually a model for these features. In conversation, we use a range of verbal and nonverbal expressions to communicate. Among the verbal forms are **phrasal verbs** and **idioms**.

Phrasal verbs

A **phrasal verb** is a regular verb followed by a preposition or adverb, such as *turn on*, *set apart*, or *get up*. The phrasal verb's meaning often cannot be guessed just by knowing the original verb. For example, we all know the meaning of *come*, but *come around* can mean *visit* or *wake up*.

4 **Work with a partner. Match the common phrasal verbs on the left with their one-word equivalents on the right.**

   a. hold back   **1.** resemble

   b. make up   **2.** tolerate

   c. point out   **3.** invent / create

   d. put up with   **4.** indicate

   e. rule out   **5.** defend

   f. run into   **6.** eliminate

   g. show up   **7.** arrive

   h. stand up for   **8.** meet (by chance)

   i. take after   **9.** convince / persuade

   j. talk into   **10.** restrain

Note: Phrasal verbs are certainly not "bad" English. However, phrasal verbs are usually more suited to conversational English, and might not be appropriate in an academic context.

Idioms

An **idiom** is a phrase that has a meaning different from the literal reading, which, if directly translated, loses either the meaning or the grammar. Here are two examples of idiomatic expressions:

a) It's raining cats and dogs.

b) The basketball player is on fire.

In a), of course it doesn't mean that cats and dogs are falling from the sky. It simply means raining heavily.

In b), the player is not literally "burning"; it means he or she is playing extremely well.

Idioms can be fun, and are perfectly acceptable in spoken English. However, they are casual in style and not usually appropriate for academic writing.

5 **Work with a partner. Guess the meaning of the following idiomatic expressions. Check your dictionary if necessary. Then rewrite the idea in more formal language.**

  a. She went off the deep end.

  b. He needs to pull his socks up.

  c. I was over the moon.

  d. The exam was a piece of cake.

  e. I passed by the skin of my teeth.

6 Work with a partner. Read the following paragraph. Circle the phrasal verbs and underline the idioms. Then rewrite it in a more appropriate academic style. Compare your new paragraph with another pair.

As a young man, he took after his father in many ways, burned the candle at both ends, and eventually became filthy rich. Although he was not the sharpest tool in the box, this did not hold him back, and his hard work paid off. Perhaps his greatest achievement was his idea to cut down on the amount of waste within local government. He had a hard time talking the local officials into going along with it, but once they started saving money hand over fist, he was the toast of the town. He gave up working soon after, but he stayed on in an advisory role right until he passed on last year.

Hedging

You may find as your research paper progresses that you still believe your original thesis, but that your argument is not quite as black and white as you first thought. You might have found information that weakens your claim, so you'd like to take a less absolute position on your argument. Take a look at the following statement:

Our continued practice of polluting water will destroy all animal life.

When the writer originally stated this, he may well have believed that this level of threat was indeed true. He may now feel, however, that such a strong statement doesn't fully reflect the facts uncovered in the research. In this case, the language can be adjusted by using hedges. Compare this version:

If we continue polluting water, it is likely that many animals will die.

A hedge can refine the shape of your argument — making it more tentative and less strict, absolute, and forceful, thereby making it easier for the reader to accept and believe.

How to use hedges

Adverbs

Sometimes you can insert an adverb or adverbial expression to soften the impact of what you are saying and make it less absolute. Here is a list of useful expressions (this is not an exhaustive list):

a little	often	rather	slightly
generally	possibly	reasonably	somewhat
moderately	probably	relatively	to some extent

Example: *Driving at night is dangerous.* ➔ *Driving at night is somewhat dangerous.*

Note: A few adverbial expressions make sentences more absolute, and less likely to be true. Avoid expressions such as *all, always, every, all of the time, never, none, nobody,* and so on.

7 **Insert an adverb into the following sentences to reflect a more tentative position. Then compare your sentences with a partner.**

   a. Smog is the cause of modern respiratory ailments.

   b. Urban air pollution causes lung cancer.

   c. Congenital defects and psychological disorders are the result of a polluted planet.

Modal verbs

Another way to soften your message is by using certain modal verbs, such as ***can, could, may, might, ought to, should***, and so on.

Example: *Driving at night is dangerous, and there will be accidents.* → *Driving at night is somewhat dangerous, and there could be accidents.*

8 **Insert a modal verb into the following sentences to reflect a more tentative position. Then compare your sentences with a partner.**

   a. Researchers in future generations will study us and our habits and wonder why we developed plastics.

   b. Human civilization will see a decline as demands for fossil fuels increase.

   c. The widespread use of petro-chemicals will someday mark the end of life.

Modifiers

Instead of suggesting that something is true ***in all cases***, it makes your argument more credible if you admit that it might not ***always*** be the case. Here you can use quantifiers like these:

a (good / high) number of a (significant) portion of few little	many most much	several some the majority / minority of

Example: *Driving at night is dangerous, and people will have an accident.* → *Driving at night is somewhat dangerous, and a good number of people could have an accident at some point in their lives.*

9 **Insert a modifier into the following sentences to reflect a more tentative position. Then compare your sentences with a partner.**

   a. Visitors to foreign lands feel free to pollute.

   b. Humans are polluters.

   c. Pollution threatens life in the biosphere.

Qualifying phrases

A well-placed qualifying phrase can make your argument seem more tentative, and this quality may add credibility to what you say. Here are some phrases:

It seems that …

Many people believe that …

There is a tendency to think that …

It is understood that …

It is possible that …

It might be the case that …

Example: *Driving at night is more dangerous than driving in the day.* → *It is possible that driving at night is more dangerous than driving in the day.*

10 **Insert a qualifying phrase into the following sentences to reflect a more tentative position. Then compare your sentences with a partner.**
    a. Pollution exists because people work and play unconsciously every day of their lives.
    b. Polluting water is like polluting yourself.
    c. Polluters have no respect for the environment.

Qualifying conditionals

Finally, you can make your claim more credible by adding a qualifying or limiting condition. The simplest way to do this is by adding an 'if' clause:

Example: *Driving at night is dangerous.* → *Driving at night is dangerous if you don't pay attention to the road and driving conditions.*

11 **Insert a qualifying conditional into the following sentences to reflect a more tentative position. Then compare your sentences with a partner.**
    a. People who pollute water should be charged with a crime.
    b. We will destroy ourselves by our waste products.
    c. Humans will need to invent new ways of breathing.

12 Work with a partner. Look at the following paragraph. Circle any examples where you think the assertion of the writer is too strong. Rewrite the paragraph on a separate piece of paper, using more tentative, hedging language. Then share your new paragraph with another pair.

Plastics are unsafe. In fact, plastics are composed of very dangerous toxins, and toxins damage the very cells of your body. They damage the endocrine system, the vital system that regulates hormones. These disruptions affect fetal development, sexual development, brain development, motor development, and are linked to a wide range of cancers. Two of the most common and yet dangerous toxins are BPA and PCBs. Through their extensive use in so many products, they are now in soil, air, and water. In fact, they are in the containers we use to hold and transport water. If we do not address this dangerous issue soon, the world will be in serious trouble.

13 Work with a partner. Look at the model research paper on pages 111–118. Can you find examples of hedging language? Note in the space provided the number you find. Then compare your results with your classmates.

....

....

....

....

....

Put it together

a Look at your research paper draft. Look to see if there are any of the following forms:

- Weak or vague language

- Phrasal verbs

- Idioms

If so, make notes in pen or pencil with more precise and academic language. Use a dictionary or ask your instructor for advice if necessary.

b Have you made any statements that are too strong or too absolute? If so, add hedges to make them more tentative.

c Write a second draft of your research paper. Consider content, organization, and language choices. You will edit for finer points when you prepare your final draft after Unit 12. As usual, save a copy of this draft in two places. You may also wish to save a copy of your earlier draft.

Your instructor may ask you to turn in a copy of your second draft. If so, print out a hard copy and turn it in; keep an additional hard copy for yourself. Remember not to leave printing till the last minute, in case there is a problem with the printer you plan to use!

▮▮ *Editing Your Paper*

In this unit you will ...
- ▦ learn how to check your own paper for language and punctuation.
- ▦ discuss issues related to accuracy in research.
- ▦ learn how to write an APA-style abstract.
- ▦ conduct a "self check" on your own paper.

I Work with a partner or group. Discuss these questions.
- How do you usually check your written work?
- How well do you think your methods work?
- What kinds of mistakes do you not catch? Why, do you think?
- What types of grammatical mistakes do you think you commonly make? How could you check for these mistakes?

Editing your work

You have already considered the content, organization, and language of your research paper. Now it is time to edit more carefully for grammar and spelling.

It isn't really possible to find grammatical errors—that is, things that are wrong, but that you do not realize are wrong. However, it is possible to find grammatical mistakes—that is, things that are wrong that you can recognize as being wrong.

One of the easiest ways to find mistakes such as subject/verb agreement errors, incorrect word forms, repeated or missing words, or faulty syntax is to read your paper out loud. Your ears will "catch" mistakes that your eyes do not.

2   **Work with a partner. Take turns reading the sentences aloud. Match the problems you find with those in the Error Box. Some sentences have more than one problem.**

Example:

<u>8, 9</u>   *The lion lie there and looked calm at Daniel.*

The adjective *calm* should be an adverb (*calmly*), and verb *lie* should be in the past tense (*lay*).

<table>
<tr>
<td colspan="5" align="center">**Error Box**</td>
</tr>
<tr>
<td>1. Pronoun reference</td>
<td>3. Missing punctuation</td>
<td>5. Misplaced comma</td>
<td>7. Apostrophe problem</td>
<td rowspan="2">9. Wrong verb tense</td>
</tr>
<tr>
<td>2. Dangling modifier</td>
<td>4. Sentence fragment</td>
<td>6. Informal language</td>
<td>8. Wrong word form</td>
<td>10. Wrong spelling or wrong word</td>
</tr>
</table>

....   **a.** Its primary weakness is the amount of water its designed to hold.

....   **b.** The new stoplight in town requires motorists to slow down when blinking.

....   **c.** To prevent dogs from chewing curtains and rugs, spray them with a fine mist of polyurethane.

....   **d.** Nora dropped the heavy, but fragile ashtray on her foot and break it.

....   **e.** Mr. Snobgoblin told his son that his Porsche had a dead battery, a broken window, and two flat tires.

....   **f.** With all of our modern advances are still unable to fight poverty.

....   **g.** Last night while studying English, a huge cockroach jumped on the television.

....   **h.** The farmers have been struggling desperately to make end meat.

....   **i.** I can't believe he asked me Where does it say in the manual that we have to wash our hands after leaving the restroom?

....   **j.** I love rice brown or white I do however have a deep-seated loathing for rice muffins.

Subject-verb agreement

Subject-verb agreement is quite simple when the subject is one word and the verb appears right after it:

The <u>man</u> <u>gives</u> a lot of money to charity.

However, it's possible for a verb to be located far away from the noun it must agree with:

The <u>man</u> whom I met last night at the event attended by several current celebrities dressed in the latest fashions <u>gives</u> a lot of money to charity.

Remember that noun clauses are usually singular:

<u>Giving a lot of money to charity</u> <u>is</u> one sign of a generous spirit.

3 **Underline the subject in each sentence once and the verb twice. Include subjects and verbs in clauses. Then change any verbs that do not agree with their subjects.**

a. Cyberbullying, a type of intimidating or harassing others through words and photos posted online, is a growing problem in some areas.

b. Even cell phone text messages has been used to bully.

c. In fact, a recent survey of American school children report that one in three kids have experienced cyberbullying.

d. Thirty percent of those children who has been cyberbullied says they were bullied through social networking sites.

e. Parents and teachers aren't always aware of the problem.

f. Some children, according to the survey, doesn't like to report the problem because of fear or embarrassment.

g. Parents, on the other hand, worries that checking their teens' online activity might be a violation of privacy.

h. However, the problems of cyberbullying is so severe that monitoring may be more important than protecting privacy, especially in the case of younger children.

Word forms

As you know, the same base word can be used in different forms as different parts of speech. *Nation* is a noun, but you can also *nationalize* a law, find a *national* version of a product, or implement a plan *nationally* or even *internationally*.

It's important to check your sentences to make sure you chose the correct form of the word. Sometimes spellcheckers, for example, might select the right spelling for you, but the wrong part of speech.

Be careful with adjective forms that come from the present participle (—*ing*) and past participle (—*ed*) of verbs. A *fascinating speaker* is one who fascinates other people; *a fascinated listener* is one who is fascinated by what he or she hears.

4   Find and correct the word form error in each of the sentences.

  a. Birth order, or the order in which children are born, can shape one's personal.

  b. Children born firstly are, not surprisingly, often leaders.

  c. They receive more of their parents' attention because there is no compete from siblings.

  d. Parents don't intention to give less attention to a second child, but necessarily they must divide their time between two children.

  e. Middle children, with an older and a younger sibling, often learn to be diplomat and flexible.

  f. The youngest child in a family is often the most creatively or artistic, but also the most insecure.

  g. Even though several research studies have found similarity personality traits that seem to be caused by birth order, other studies have found no such effects.

  h. Although the idea that your birth order determines your personality is interested, bear in mind that other, stronger influences also affect your personality.

Accuracy in research and writing

Previously, you examined the issue of plagiarism, one type of writing "crime." Now, read the story of reporter Stephen Glass about another type of writing crime, falsification.

Stephen Glass (American, 1972–) is one of the best-known modern examples of journalistic fraud. After graduating from the University of Pennsylvania, where he had worked as the executive editor of the student newspaper, he took a job in 1995 as a reporter for the prestigious magazine *The New Republic*. He was 23 years old. While working full-time for *The New Republic*, Glass also wrote freelance articles for a number of other well-known publications, including *Policy Review*, *Rolling Stone*, and *Harper's*.

As early as 1996, various individuals and organizations challenged the truthfulness and accuracy of several of Glass' articles; however, Glass denied any wrong-doing, and his editors at *The New Republic* backed him up. After all, Glass reported on sensitive and controversial topics, and it perhaps was not surprising that those he criticized would be upset.

It was Glass' article "Hack Heaven," which appeared in the May 18, 1998 issue of *The New Republic*, that caused his eventual downfall. The story concerned a 15-year old computer hacker named Ian Restil who broke into the computer network of a company called Jukt Micronics—who were so impressed with Restil's skills that they hired him as a security consultant.

Problem: Ian Restil didn't exist. And neither did Jukt Micronics. Adam Penenberg, a reporter for *Forbes* magazine, who also covered computer hackers, was suspicious about the story and conducted his own investigation. When he called *The New Republic* with his findings, Glass at first tried to cover his tracks, claiming that Restil had misled him. Eventually, however, the extent of Glass' fraud was uncovered. At that point, *The New Republic* took a closer look at previous Glass work, and found that at least 27 out of 41 articles he had written contained information that had been simply made up.

Stephen Glass lost his job at *The New Republic*, though he went on to earn a law degree from Georgetown University, and also wrote a fictionalized account of his career in 2003 called *The Fabulist*. *Shattered Glass*, a movie account of his work at *The New Republic*, including details of the investigation that uncovered his fraud, was also released in 2003.

Stephen Glass' story raises many questions. Why did he do it? How could he think he would get away with it? Why, in fact, did he get away with it for so long? Commenting on Glass' career in both journalism and fiction, Penenberg remarked: "With *The Fabulist*, Stephen Glass published fiction when he should have published fact; with his magazine articles, he gave us fiction when he should have published fact. In Glass's fabricated world, sources say the most incredible things and he is witness to events that are almost too good to be true (because they weren't). Unfortunately, reality is rarely so neat and interesting—and perhaps that's the problem. It's hard work being a journalist; it's far easier to create stories out of thin air. It's why journalists shun Glass now. He cheated, and when he got caught, he made all of us look bad. But what is saddest perhaps is that in *The Fabulist*, when Glass had the chance to let his creativity flow, all he could come up with was thinly veiled fiction. That's not very creative" (2011).

5 **Work in a group. Discuss these questions.**

- Why might a reporter write false information? List as many reasons as you can think of. Are some reasons more "justifiable" than others?

- Who has the responsibility for ensuring that articles in newspapers and magazines are true? How can they accomplish this?

- What are some reasons that stories with incorrect or falsified information still get into print?

- Some people will only allow themselves to be interviewed if they can remain anonymous. What impact does this have on fact-checking? Should anonymous sources ever be believed? Should reporters be required to reveal the identities of anonymous sources?

6 | *Optional outside assignment*

Work with a partner or a small group. Investigate one of the people listed below. Explain to the class the controversy surrounding the person's research and/or writing. Do you think the person you chose was guilty of any wrongdoing? Why or why not?

Alex Haley / *Roots*	Jayson Blair	Stephen Glass
Dan Brown / *The DaVinci Code*	Kaavya Viswanathan	Stephen King / *Desperation*
Doris Kearns Goodwin	Rick Bragg	Yann Martel
Gerald Posner	Stephen Ambrose	

Abstracts

In a formal APA-style research paper, the abstract serves as a summary of the key points of your paper. As part of the academic community, you can help your fellow researchers by writing a concise and informative abstract.

An abstract is a summary or overview of your paper, placed after the title page and before the body of your paper. When your work is published, it is often the first thing that people will read. The most common kind of abstract includes brief details such as a reference to the main problem or related background, the main point of the research, key discoveries within the research paper, and conclusions or suggestions for future action. Present the information in the same order that you chose for your research paper.

Different academic organizations, conferences, journals, and professors will specify the word limit for abstracts. Ask your instructor what the word limit is for your paper. In general, abstracts are between 120 and 250 words long. Take your time; abstracts are important, and you may find it is harder than you think to write all the details you need within a very tight word limit.

Look at the example from the model research paper you have been studying in this course. (In the final draft of a submitted paper, the abstract, like the body of the paper, will be double-spaced. Here it is single-spaced to save room.)

Abstract

This paper investigates whether sugar, especially refined sugar so prevalent in food nowadays, is more of a health risk than a health benefit. Sugar can be found, both naturally and artificially, in almost all aspects of the modern diet, and the over-consumption of sugar is a cause for concern in the modern world. The paper examines the origins of sugar in the human diet and then considers some of the nutritional properties of sugar. Based on the conclusions of various scientific research papers, it is argued that sugar, especially in its refined state, is responsible for creating a vicious cycle of consumption and a range of disturbing conditions and illnesses. The paper concludes by strongly suggesting that everybody should reflect on their diet and, if need be, reduce their sugar intake in order to maintain a healthy life.

7 Work with a partner. Underline the following in the abstract on page 90:

- Related background information, or a main problem
- The main point of the research
- Key discoveries
- Conclusions or suggestions for future action

8 Work with a partner. Answer the questions without referring to your research paper. Then write your answers on a separate sheet of paper. These should help you write your abstract.

    a. What problem, or issue, or general background information helped you choose your topic?

    b. What is the main purpose of your research?

    c. What are the main discoveries you made through the course of your research?

    d. What are your conclusions, or suggestions for future action?

9 Write a draft of your abstract.

10 Read your draft aloud to a partner. If your partner understands exactly what your paper is about, your abstract has done its job. If not, you will need to refine it. Ask your partner what he or she did not understand. Then make any necessary revisions to your abstract.

Put it together

a Read your paper aloud. Mark any mistakes that you find.

b Check for subject-verb agreement: Underline the subject of each sentence once, and the verb twice. Do they agree?

c Check your nouns, verbs, adjectives, and adverbs. Have you used the correct form?

d Note any necessary changes on a hard copy of your paper; or, if you have time, make them electronically. You will turn in a final copy of your research paper after Unit 12.

12 *Presenting Your Research*

In this unit you will …

- ■ prepare for and deliver an oral presentation of your research.
- ■ learn how to format an APA-style title page.
- ■ learn how to format an APA-style Works Cited section.
- ■ submit your final research paper.

I Discuss these questions in a group.

- How do you like to give and receive information about a classmate's research: through a presentation, or in an informal group discussion?

- Tell the group about one good and one poor presentation you've attended. What made them good or bad?

- Do you get nervous when you give presentations? What are some things presenters can do to help them deal with nerves?

- During a presentation, what is the role of the audience? What are audience members' responsibilities?

Preparing a short presentation

You have worked hard in this course researching a topic in depth and formulating your insights and ideas. Now it is your chance to shine as a researcher. Talking about your experiences as a researcher is the climax of the story of research. You have read a great deal, written and rewritten, and talked to others about your research project while gathering new perspectives. Talking is a simple but important way to deepen the understanding you have of your project.

A short presentation is one effective way to crystallize your ideas, give them life beyond the written page, and to get some immediate responses.

Your presentation will cover only the main points of your research; you are not going to (and don't have time to) read your entire paper aloud. Instead, showcase the highlights of your research by summarizing the main ideas and the most interesting and convincing supporting points. In most cases, you would include every main point from each body paragraph—but not always! It depends on the length of your paper and, of course, on the importance of each point. Referring back to your abstract is an easy way to find the main points of your research.

Note how the main points are arranged in the following presentation outline for the research paper on sugar:

Point 1 – The hook: Sugar is a dangerous and pervasive poison.

Point 2 – Thesis: People should be aware of the dangers of eating too much sugar and should take steps to reduce the amount of sugar in their diet.

Point 3 – Sugar's historical uses

Point 4 – Sugar's widespread uses today

Point 5 – The manufacturing and processing of sugar

Point 6 – Sugar's connection to disease

Point 7 – Sugar's destructive potential

Point 8 – Conclusion: Urge audience to consume less sugar.

2 **Work with a partner. Refer to your outline. Choose the main ideas that you both feel would be relevant and useful to the short presentation. Mark any supporting information that you think is essential or interesting. It is important that you receive some feedback from your partner as you select the points for your presentation.**

Using notes in a presentation

It is not very interesting to watch someone read a paper aloud. Your audience would much rather have you just talk to them. However, it can be difficult to remember everything you want to say, especially if you wish to use some direct quotes (or if you get very nervous when you present!).

It is less distracting to your audience if you speak from note cards or from Powerpoint slides (which are, after all, a type of notecard). If you use paper cards, write one main point on each card. Include important supporting information on other cards. Carefully number your cards to keep them in order.

Practice speaking from your cards so that you learn to glance down at your card, take in the information, and look up to speak. If you must read from a card—for example, to read a long quotation—don't hold the card directly in front of your eyes or mouth. Instead, hold it out away from your body a bit.

Presentation software (such as Powerpoint) slides are popular in presentations too. Use these to display charts, graphs, photographs, and other visual information, or to show your main points to your audience. Keep any text short, almost like a slogan. If you put exactly the same text on the slide that you intend to say, there is no reason for your audience to listen to you!

Remember: If you use presentation software, be sure to test your equipment well in advance of your presentation.

3 Check (✓) the behaviors that you think make a good presentation. Then compare your responses in a group. Are there other features that you like to see in a presentation?

☐ asking the audience questions   ☐ telling a few jokes

☐ dressing nicely   ☐ using a formal speaking style

☐ facing the audience   ☐ using an informal speaking style

☐ giving a quiz after the presentation   ☐ using handouts

☐ quoting research directly   ☐ using music during a slide presentation

☐ showing pictures or other visual aids   ☐ using notecards

☐ speaking quickly   ☐ using presentation software

☐ speaking slowly

Audience participation

You are expected, of course, to listen to your classmates' presentation. This is your chance to see the results of their research. One way to show that you have been paying attention is by asking questions and making comments. Of course, your questions and comments should be both polite and relevant. It's best to ask questions at the end of a presentation, since a question you have in the middle of a presentation might get answered later on. If you think you might forget your question, make notes as you listen.

As the presenter, you may be asked questions that you cannot answer. There is (usually!) no reason to be embarrassed by this. Simply say, "I'm sorry, I didn't come across that information in my research," or "I'm afraid I don't know the answer to that question."

4   **Work with a partner. Check (✓) the appropriate questions and comments. Discuss why the ones you didn't check are not appropriate.**

- [ ] **a.** Could you repeat your second main point?
- [ ] **b.** I agree with what you said about birth order. In fact, I'm a middle child, and in my family …
- [ ] **c.** What song was playing during your presentation? Could I borrow that CD?
- [ ] **d.** We were supposed to talk for five minutes, but you spoke for seven.
- [ ] **e.** Can you show that slide of the bar chart again? I didn't understand what it was showing.
- [ ] **f.** Is what you said about whales also true for dolphins or any other large sea creatures?
- [ ] **g.** How long did it take you to draw those pictures?
- [ ] **h.** Do you think there's anything that we can do personally to fight against overpopulation, or is it only a problem for governments?
- [ ] **i.** Have you stopped eating so much sugar since you learned this information?
- [ ] **j.** How come you didn't quote any experts during your presentation?

Your instructor will schedule oral presentations for your class. In some cases, you may give your presentation before you turn in your final draft; however, your research and writing have already been completed.

Preparing the final draft

In addition to making any final changes to language, and carefully proofreading your paper for mistakes and proper formatting, there are two more things to add to your research paper before it is complete: a title page and a References section.

Title page

The title page acts as an invitation to readers. As you might expect, style guides, such as the *APA Style Manual*, follow a standard format. Notice the format in the following example. Note that all characters are in the same font style and size as the research paper. (Your title page will take up an entire page; here, the example is on a shorter page to save space.)

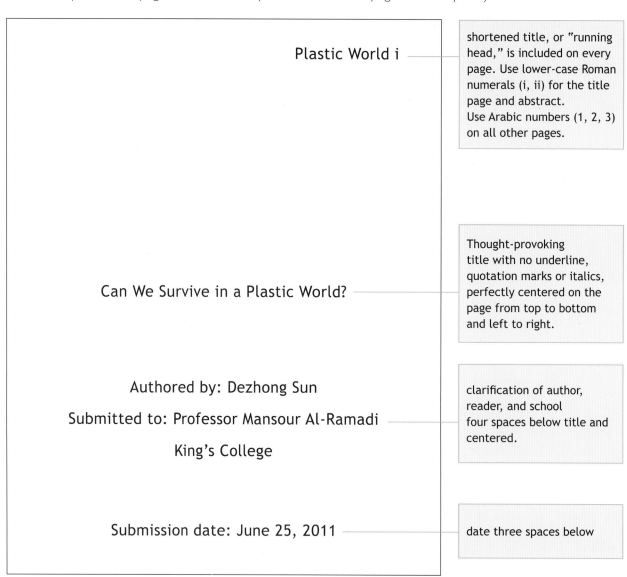

Plastic World i — shortened title, or "running head," is included on every page. Use lower-case Roman numerals (i, ii) for the title page and abstract. Use Arabic numbers (1, 2, 3) on all other pages.

Can We Survive in a Plastic World? — Thought-provoking title with no underline, quotation marks or italics, perfectly centered on the page from top to bottom and left to right.

Authored by: Dezhong Sun
Submitted to: Professor Mansour Al-Ramadi — clarification of author, reader, and school four spaces below title and centered.
King's College

Submission date: June 25, 2011 — date three spaces below

References

Publication details recorded in the References section (also known as a bibliography) should be consistent, and the formatting of those details should be complete and correct. This part of the research process can be tedious, but it is still very important. You might think of the bibliography as a library in itself. It is a very convenient list that contains details about where you have gone as a researcher to learn and to gather new information, and it allows an interested reader to find that same information.

5 Work with a partner. The key contains most of the major aspects that appear in most sources. Use it to label each part of the following references.

Key		
A. author(s)	F. journal name	K. database name
B. editor(s)	G. year of publication	L. page numbers
C. translator(s)	H. date of publication	M. publisher
D. book/magazine title	I. date of retrieval	N. city of publication
E. article/chapter title	J. volume/issue number	O. web address

Arrighi, G. (1996). *The long twentieth century: Money, power, and the origins of our times.* New York: Verso.

Bourdieu, P., & Passeron, J. C. (1977). *Reproduction in education, society and culture* (L. J. D. Wacquant, Trans.). London: Sage Publications.

Caruso, E. M., Mead, N. L., & Balcetis, E. (2009). Political partisanship influences perception of biracial candidates' skin tone. *Proceedings of the National Academy of Sciences of the United States.* 106 (48) pp. 20168-20173.

Fairclough, N. L. (1998). Political discourse in the media: An analytical framework. In A. Bell & P. Garrett (Eds.) *Approaches to Media Discourse* (pp. 142-161). Oxford: Blackwell Publishers Ltd.

Hedges, C. (2009, May 4). Buying brand Obama. *Truthdig.* Retrieved October 2, 2009 From http://www.truthdig.com/report/item/20090503buying_brand_

6 The following list, though not exhaustive, contains eight popular source types. Compare your sources to the list, and label each one with the particular source type. Then prepare a reference entry for each of your sources. Check them with a partner.

SOURCE TYPE	Bibliography
(Website)	Adger, C. T. (1997). Language policy and public knowledge. *Center for Applied Linguistics*. Retrieved September 10, 2003, from CAL database at http://www.cal.org/ebonics/eboped.htm
(Book)	Aitchison, J. (1991). *Language change: Process or decay?* Cambridge: Cambridge University Press.
(Translated book)	Barthes, R. (1999). *Elements of semiology* (A. Lavers & C. Smith, Trans.). New York: Hill and Wang. (Original work published 1964).
(Scholarly journal article)	Barker, V., & Giles, H. (2004). English-only policies: Perceived support and social limitation. *Language and Communication, 24*(1), 77-95.
(Chapter in an edited book)	Bauer, L. (1998). You shouldn't say 'it is me' because 'me' is accusative. In L. Bauer & P. Trudgill (Eds.), *Language myths* (pp. 132-138). London: Penguin.
(Magazine article)	Berry, W. (2002, November 14). Two minds. *The Progressive, 66*(11), 21-29.
(Newspaper article online)	Blakeston, R. (2002, November 21). Why do Britons Waive the Rules? Retrieved from http://guardian.co.uk/education/2002/nov/21/tefl.wordsandlanguage
(Online scholarly journal article)	Klaehn, J., & Mullen, A. (2010). *Synaesthesia: Communication across cultures*, 1(1). Retrieved from http://www.synaesthesiajournal.com/volume_1_issue_1.html

Put it together

a   Type a title page for your research paper.

b   Insert a running head at the top of each of your pages. Make sure they are numbered correctly. Remember that the abstract comes directly after the title page, before the body of your paper.

c   Conduct a final check of your paper.

- Run your computer's spell check.

- Check minor formatting: Does every sentence begin with a capital letter and close with appropriate end punctuation?

- Did you use a standard 12-point font? Did you leave a 1 cm space on every margin? Did you double-space the text?

d   Create a References section for your paper. Make sure that every source you used is listed, even if you did not use in-text citations from some of them. Alphabetize the references.

e   Work with a group. Discuss the questions.

- What was easy for you about writing this research paper? What was challenging?

- What is something you think you did well?

- What is something you would do differently next time?

- What are two more topics you would enjoy researching?

Finally, shake the hands of your fellow group members. Congratulations! You are now both a researcher–and a writer.

NASAA

| ABOUT NASAA | INVESTOR EDUCATION | ISSUES & ANSWERS | NASAA NEWSROOM | INDUSTRY & REGULATORY SERVICES |

IN THIS SECTION

• Current NASAA Headlines

• News Release Archive

• News from the Regulators

• Speeches

• What's New

• NASAA Forums

• NASAA Annual Report

• Speakers Bureau

• NASAA Insight

SEARCH   sitemap

[   ] GO

QUICKLINKS

• Contact Your Regulator

• What's New

• Member Login

• E-mail Updates

printer-friendly page

Current NASAA Headlines

October 20, 2010

NASAA Urges Caution for Investors Mining for Golden Opportunities

Massey: "It is a myth to say that gold is a safe investment."

WASHINGTON (October 20, 2010) – With gold prices reaching record highs, investors are increasingly turning to gold-related investments. The North American Securities Administrators Association (NASAA) today reminded investors to be cautious about jumping onto the gold bandwagon.

"The soaring price of gold has sparked a modern-day gold rush among investors eager to recover stock market losses. But it's still a Wild West out there and dangers abound for prospective gold investors," said David Massey, NASAA President and North Carolina Deputy Securities Administrator.

State and provincial securities regulators have issued an alert to help investors spot the risks of gold investments.

"It is a myth to say that gold is a safe investment. An investment in gold is not foolproof," Massey said. "An investor needs to know his or her investment objectives. Gold may not provide long-term investment returns. Gold is a commodity, and, like other commodities, its price can fluctuate dramatically."

Historically speaking, the value of gold-related investments fluctuates even more than the stock market. Gold often moves in reverse of stocks and bonds, so when stocks are down, gold may seem like a very tempting investment.

There are many ways to invest in gold, including buying actual gold or making gold-related market investments in mutual funds, exchange-traded funds and futures, as well as shares of gold mining companies. NASAA's investor alert examines each of these options and explains what investors need to know about each before deciding to invest.

NASAA also advises investors to beware of gold investment scams. For example, in one typical scheme, a seller offers to sell actual gold bullion and then retain the investor's gold in a "secure" vault with a promise to sell the gold for the investor as it gains in value. In many instances, the gold does not exist. In another typical scenario, a company encourages investors to cash out of their poor-performing investments to purchase gold, which may be nothing more than "fool's gold."

"Remember, if you are advised to cash out investments and roll funds into a different type of investment, make sure the person advising this is licensed by your state securities regulator," Massey said.

The investor alert is available on the NASAA website at www.nasaa.org.

NASAA is the oldest international organization devoted to investor protection. Its membership consists of the securities administrators in the 50 states, the District of Columbia, Puerto Rico, the U.S. Virgin Islands, Canada and Mexico.

Online Investing AI

Online Investing AI

Realize massive trading profits as advanced artificial intelligence technology trades for you.

More money. Less risk. Absolute freedom.

Have you ever tried any of the following?

- **Swing** trading
- **Forex** trading
- **Automated** Trading
- **Hedge** Trading

New trading systems and auto trading technology have revolutionized investing. Traders have access to an entire universe of investments. They can trade 24 hours a day. They can trade anywhere they want. They can trade multiple strategies.

So why aren't more traders fabulously wealthy?

It's because auto trading systems are just that – static systems. And systems don't change, even when the markets do.

To earn exponential returns, at a lower risk, we created an advanced trading intelligence platform.

Online Investing AI is one of the first trading intelligence that uses advanced AI (Artificial Intelligence), genetic programming, and trading technologies to "learn" the market, so you earn more money with less risk.

Over 1,000 hours of hard core computer computations have gone into developing our automated trading intelligence platform.

Stay updated with the latest info.

Your email: [   ]

[Subscribe]   [Unsubscribe]

We will ...

Peer review form essay:

Name:

Classmate's name:

Title of classmate's essay:

Date:

1. What is the topic?

2. Is the essay expository or persuasive?

3. Write the thesis statement here:

....

....

4. How many body paragraphs are there?

5. Does the introduction have a hook? .... What other information is in the introduction?

6. Underline the topic sentence in each body paragraph. If you can't find one, note it here:

7. Write the number of each body paragraph and then explain what types of support were used for each paragraph. (Check for a list of types on page 5.)

....

....

....

....

....

....

8. Does the conclusion tie back to the introduction? .... What functions does the conclusion fulfill?

....

....

9. Write a question mark (?) by anything in the essay that you didn't understand. Write a short note to explain if possible.

10. On the essay, draw a star (*) by the two sentences you liked best.

11. Any other comments: ....

....

....

....

....

....

Peer review form research paper:

Writer's name: ....

Reviewer's name: ....

Title of the research paper: ....

Date: ....

General

1. What is the topic of the paper? ....
2. Underline the thesis statement on the paper.
3. In your own words, what is the thesis? ....

....

4. How many main ideas are there?

....

5. Is the paper persuasive or expository?

....

Introduction

1. Does the introduction begin with a hook? If so, what kind of hook?

....

2. Does the introduction include background information? If so, about what?

....

3. Is the thesis statement the final sentence of the introduction? ....

Body

1. How many body paragraphs are there? ....
2. Underline the topic sentence in each body paragraph.
3. For each body paragraph, write the types of support that appear (e.g., statistics, results of a study, expert testimony, personal experience, logical reasoning, etc).

....

....

....

....

....

....

....

....

4. How are the body paragraphs arranged? (e.g., chronologically; least important to most important idea; no particular order)

....

....

5. Which piece of research do you find the most convincing?

....

....

6. Is there any research that you think does not support the author's point? If so, explain here:

....

....

....

....

7. Are there any points that you feel need more support? If so, explain here:

....

....

....

....

Conclusion

1. Does the conclusion tie back to the introduction? If so, how?

....

....

....

2. Does the conclusion summarize the main points?

....

3. Are any new points raised in the conclusion? If so, what?

....

....

....

4. What else does the conclusion do? (eg, make a prediction or recommendation)

....

General impressions

1. What are two things you learned from reading this paper?

....

....

....

2. Draw a star (*) by your two favorite sentences in the paper.

Sample essay

Ji-un Kang

English Composition 101

March 15, 2011

I really like your title. It's clever and really represents the content of the essay. The title asks readers to consider whether sugar is good or bad, and then develops a discussion around these points. Very nice!

Sugar: Friend or Foe?

In the developed world, sugar is present in almost all aspects of our diet. The most common sources of natural sugar are sugar cane and the sugar beet. Sugar also occurs naturally in most fruits and some other foods. However, in addition to these natural sugars, there is a huge amount of refined sugar added to the food and drink we consume. Soft drinks, sweets, desserts, fast food, and even salty foods like crisps all contain some form of sugar added to make them taste better. The results of this over-consumption of sugar are worrying. It is linked to obesity, tooth decay, diabetes, and other illnesses and conditions. People should be aware of the amount of sugar in their diets and take steps to reduce it.

ink this is sive voice. professor we should aware of the ce we use. you mean mphasize w sugar" re than the mans" who it? Maybe do.

Our professor says we're supposed to highlight the thesis of the essay. So, I choose this line. I hope I'm right.

Raw sugar has been eaten by humans for thousands of years. Sugar is a form of pure energy, high in calories and low in nutrients. Like gasoline refined from raw crude oil, refined sugar has undergone a process to make it easy to store, transport, and consume. Refined sugar fuels the body with instant energy, while also having a pleasant taste. In fact, it is this pleasant taste that is the problem. The appealing taste can make a person want to consume more, even when the body is at rest and has no need of sugar. Over-filling a car with gasoline creates only a minor spill at the local filling station, but over-filling a human with sugar can create much greater problems.

I'm sorry, I'm not sure why you're talking about a gas station here.

One of the greatest dangers of consuming too much refined sugar is obesity. Many college students in Japan and Korea, for example, report that they gain weight during their studies abroad in North America and Western Europe. There could be many reasons for this, but one primary cause is eating too much sugar. Visitors to these regions are often surprised at both how common sweets are and how sweet the foods are. In fact, when the typical sugar content of the average diet in North America is compared with that of most Asian or Middle Eastern countries, the difference is clear. This corresponds to a similar difference in rates of obesity, particularly among children. Obesity in turn can lead to many other problems, including heart disease and depression.

In addition to obesity, refined sugar is responsible for a rise in other modern conditions and illnesses such as diabetes, tooth decay, and gout. By changing our sugar-eating habits, we can reduce the occurrence of these serious ailments.

Finally, over-consumption of refined sugar steals nutrients from the body. The body's engine, the metabolism, has great difficulty burning refined sugars, and so it must use some of its own stored nutrients to convert refined sugars into energy. This is why refined sugar has been called a thief.

In conclusion, instead of being a useful fuel for the body, refined sugar acts like the body's enemy. Of course, as with all things in life, raw sugar in moderation is both healthy and desirable. However, with the high concentrations of refined sugars in so many common products, eating sugar only in moderation is a big challenge. Everyone needs to face this challenge and recognize how serious it is.

Is it really "many" students? Maybe you could make this more tentative.

This is a very interesting observation, wonder if it could be supported with reference evidence.

This feels more like a topic sentence than a concluding sentence.

This is a good topic sentence, but you only devote a single line to its discussion. I wonder if you could expand on this point with some evidence and discussion?

These paragraphs are a little short. Could you find some way to join them together? Or maybe you want to expand them a little?

This is a nice closing line because, like a good call to action, it challenges readers to be more thoughtful about what they eat.

Sample essay final version

Ji-un Kang

English Composition 101

March 15, 2011

Sugar: Friend or Foe?

In the developed world, sugar is present in almost all aspects of our diet. The most common sources of natural sugar are sugar cane and the sugar beet. Sugar also occurs naturally in most fruits and some other foods. However, in addition to these natural sugars, there is a huge amount of refined sugar added to the food and drink we consume. Soft drinks, sweets, desserts, fast food, and even salty foods like crisps all contain some form of sugar added to make them taste better. The results of this over-consumption of sugar are worrying. It is linked to obesity, tooth decay, diabetes, and other illnesses and conditions. People should be aware of the amount of sugar in their diets and take steps to reduce it.

Raw sugar has been eaten by humans for thousands of years. Sugar is a form of pure energy, high in calories and low in nutrients. Like gasoline refined from raw crude oil, refined sugar has undergone a process to make it easy to store, transport, and consume. Refined sugar fuels the body with instant energy, while also having a pleasant taste. In fact, it is this pleasant taste that is the problem. The appealing taste can make a person want to consume more, even when the body is at rest and has no need of sugar. Over-filling your system with this refined fuel can create some grave problems.

One of the greatest dangers of consuming too much refined sugar is obesity. A number of college students in Japan and Korea, for example, report that they gain weight during their studies abroad in North America and Western Europe. There could be many reasons for this, but one primary cause is eating too much sugar. Visitors to these regions are often surprised at both how common sweets are and how sweet the foods are. In fact, when the typical sugar content of the average diet in North America is compared with that of most Asian or Middle Eastern countries, the difference is clear. This corresponds to a similar difference in rates of obesity, particularly among children. Refined sugar, then, is clearly linked to obesity.

In addition to obesity, refined sugar is responsible for a rise in other modern conditions and illnesses such as diabetes, tooth decay, and gout. News reports about the cost of diabetes to the economic health of the nation, for example, can be seen and read almost everyday in the media. Furthermore, over-consumption of refined sugar steals nutrients from the body. The body's engine, the metabolism, has great difficulty burning refined sugars, and so it must use some of its own stored nutrients to convert refined sugars into energy. This is why refined sugar has been called a thief. By changing our sugar-eating habits, we can reduce the occurrence of these serious problems and ailments.

Instead of being a useful fuel for the body, refined sugar acts like the body's enemy. Of course, as with all things in life, raw sugar in moderation is both healthy and desirable. However, with the high concentrations of refined sugars in so many common products, eating sugar only in moderation is a big challenge. Ultimately, everyone needs to face this challenge and recognize how serious it is.

Freewriting

Freewriting is one way to help you explore the possibilities of a topic. Write about your topic without worrying about organization, grammar, vocabulary, or spelling. The purpose of the exercise is to generate as many ideas as you can.

Look at the example. Notice how the writer moves from generalities to specifics, from personal observations to global questions about how the topic may affect people. Notice, too, how the final observation she makes can lead to further exploration.

Freewriting on Sugar

I love sugar, love it and wonder sometimes why I do so much, my mother used to say I ate way too much as a child, said sugar was my only fuel. I was always filled with energy, even more than brothers were. Mom would sometimes caution me, pointing to my aunt who'd died of too much sugar consumption apparently. ~~Candys~~ Candies, cookies, chocolates, or cakes often piled high on her kitchen table for us kids when we'd come over to visit, and what did she get for the mountains of sweets she'd invite us to climb and eat? Obesity and diabetes and a lost limb and an early grave, I wonder how sugar affects people throughout the world, the world such a huge place for so, so, so much sugar. How does it give energy to the people of cultures beyond my own? What's the most popular form - raw, refined? Where are on earth are the most efficient consumers of sugar? America? Europe? Africa? Asia? My geography professor once said that sugar is the staple that holds many cultures in the Middle East together. Most of my friends who went to study in Europe and America returned home carrying heavier weight and wearing tighter jeans. I know I have to cut my sugar intake too, but don't really know why, why, why sugar has such a bad name.

Freewriting: edited version

~~I love sugar, love it and wonder sometimes why I do so much~~, my mother used to say I ate way

too much as a child, said sugar was my only <u>fuel</u>. I was always filled with energy, ~~even more than~~

Could use this idea of "fuel for the body"

~~brothers were.~~ Mom would sometimes caution me, pointing to my aunt who'd <u>died of too much</u>

I wonder i[f] this is real[ly] true. Can t[oo] much suga[r] kill you? C[an] this be a th[esis] statement?

<u>sugar consumption apparently</u>. ~~Candys Candies, cookies, chocolates, or cakes often piled high on~~

~~her kitchen table for us kids when we'd come over to visit, and what did she get for the mountains~~

~~of sweets she'd invite us to climb and eat?~~ Obesity and diabetes and a lost limb and an early

Definitely want t[o] explore these som[e] more

grave, I wonder how sugar affects people throughout the world, ~~the world such a huge place for~~

~~so, so, so much sugar.~~ How does it give energy to the people of cultures beyond my own? What's

efficient? Better at who consum[es] most.

the most popular form - <u>raw, refined</u>? Where are on earth are the most efficient consumers of

Should find about this. Actually, what exactly is refined sugar?

sugar? America? Europe? Africa? Asia? My geography professor once said that sugar is the

staple that holds many cultures in the Middle East together. Most of my friends who went to

study in Europe and America <u>returned home carrying heavier weight</u> and wearing tighter jeans. I

So I guess I [?] that N. Am[.] and Europe[?] consume m[?] sugar …

know I have to <u>cut my sugar intake</u> too, but don't really know why, ~~why, why~~ <u>sugar has such a bad</u>

<u>name.</u>

Maybe everybody needs to … poss. conclusion!

research question!

Sugar: Friend or Foe?

Authored by: Ji-un Kang

Submitted to: Professor Dorothy Zemach

Korea National University

Submission date: July 10, 2011

Abstract

This paper investigates whether sugar, especially refined sugar so prevalent in food nowadays, is more of a health risk than a health benefit. Sugar can be found, both naturally and artificially, in almost all aspects of the modern diet, and the over-consumption of sugar is a cause for concern in the modern world. The paper examines the origins of sugar in the human diet and then considers some of the nutritional properties of sugar. Based on the conclusions of various scientific research papers, it is argued that sugar, especially in its refined state, is responsible for creating a vicious cycle of consumption and a range of disturbing conditions and illnesses. The paper concludes by strongly suggesting that everybody should reflect on their diet and, if need be, reduce their sugar intake in order to maintain a healthy life.

In the developed world, sugar is present in almost all aspects of our diet. The most obvious sources of natural sugar are sugar cane and the sugar beet. Sugar also occurs naturally in most fruits, as well as in some nuts, roots, and vegetables. However, in addition to these natural sugars, there is a huge amount of refined sugar artificially inserted into our food and drink. Soft drinks, sweets, desserts, fast food, and even typically salty foods like crisps all contain some form of sugar added to make them taste better. The results of this over-consumption of sugar are linked to obesity, which can lead to diabetes, tooth decay, and a range of other illnesses and conditions. People should be aware of the dangers of eating too much sugar and should take steps to reduce the amount of sugar in their diet.

Since raw sugars appear to provide people with necessary bursts of energy, they have probably been eaten by humans in various forms for thousands of years. In fact, the cultivation of sugar likely spread throughout Southeast Asia during prehistoric times (Gascoigne, 2001). Raw sugar is a form of pure power, high in calories and almost completely stripped of any nutritional value. 100g of granulated sugar, for example, contains approximately 1,619 kJ of energy, or 387 calories, but 0g of fat, protein, or dietary fibre (USDA nutrient database, 2010). Just as gasoline is refined from raw crude oil, refined sugar has undergone a process to remove any impurities from the sugar plants, leaving almost 100% pure sugar, or sucrose.

While refined sugar fuels the body with instant energy, it also provides a pleasant taste. In fact, it is this pleasant taste that, researchers suspect, is at the root of the problem. Like an addictive drug, sugar acts on areas of the brain that control pleasure (Kelley & Berridge, 2002, p. 3307), but not all pleasures are good for the body. In his article "Sugar is a poison," Jeffrey Norris (2009) cites Dr. Robert Lustig who says that sugar makes the brain think it is hungry, setting up a vicious cycle. So, the highly appealing taste increases the craving for more—even when the human body is at rest and has no need of sugar. As fitness expert David Kirschen notes, the refining process creates certain disadvantages, especially "the stripping away of nutrients and the high concentration of empty calories," and this "can actually trigger appetite further" (2010). Eating too much sugar, then, leads to eating even more sugar, which can create significant problems.

One of the greatest dangers of consuming too much refined sugar, or sugary foods, is obesity. The official website of the World Health Organisation (2010, para. 4) states that obesity is "abnormal or excessive fat accumulation that presents a risk to health." The same website estimates that approximately two billion adults worldwide are either overweight or obese, and a staggering 80.5% of American males aged 15 and over are obese today. There is a clear link between sugar and obesity, since the high levels of energy that are contained in sugary foods, if not burned off through exercise, lead to weight gain. The health risks associated with obesity are very serious; a 2006 study (Haslam & James) of obesity concluded that "Average life expectancy is already diminished; the main adverse consequences are cardiovascular disease, type 2 diabetes, and several cancers." To avoid these negative effects, it is crucial that people do their best to avoid obesity—and that means avoiding sugar.

Furthermore, refined sugar is partly responsible for a range of conditions and illnesses that have become much more widespread and noticeable in modern society. For example, a study carried out by Vecchia, Franceschi, Bidoli, Barbone, and Dolara (1993) found that even sugar in small amounts, such as the sugar that is put in tea or coffee, has an impact on the risk of developing cancers of the digestive system. Sugar is also implicated in the development of type 2 diabetes. Although there is no direct causal link between sugar consumption and diabetes (for the causes of diabetes, see the American Dietetic Association website), weight gain and obesity—results of consuming too much sugar—put people more at risk of developing diabetes (Eberhardt et. al., 2004). According to the British charity Diabetes UK (2009, para. 4), untreated diabetes can cause weight loss, blurred vision, and many other serious symptoms. For this reason alone, the amount of sugar in the diet should be considered very carefully.

There are other health problems associated with sugar. Sugar is bad for teeth, and is a major cause of tooth decay. A study carried out in both rural and urban populations in South Africa, published on the World Health Organisation bulletin board, concluded that "high consumption of added sugars contributes significantly to the incidence of dental caries" (2003). In addition, research published in the British Medical Journal tentatively concludes that "consumption of sugar sweetened soft drinks and fructose is strongly associated with an increased risk of gout in men" (Choi & Curhan, 2008). In short, too much sugar is responsible not only for major health risks but also painful and problematic conditions.

Finally, one more issue associated with the over-consumption of refined sugar is that it steals nutrients from the body. The body's engine, the metabolism, has great difficulty burning refined sugars and so must use some of its own stored nutrients to convert refined sugars to energy. According to physical training expert Ralph Klisiewicz, refined sugar

> ... leaches the reserve of vitamins and minerals stored in your body ... Refined sugar [also] increase[s] acidity in the body. To neutralize this acid state, the body draws calcium from bones and teeth making them weaker and more susceptible to degeneration. (2010, para. 7)

These negative effects are one reason why refined sugar has been called a thief. Besides stealing, a thief can also destroy things. "Refined sugar," Klisiewicz goes on to say, "invades the lymphatic system, ... [and] results in increased white blood cell production" (2010, para. 8). Because of these effects, people are more open to other kinds of attacks from disease.

In conclusion, sugar is not an ideal fuel for the body. Instead, it acts more like the body's enemy. It causes weight gain and obesity, which can lead to many serious illnesses, as well as death. Sugar appears to be responsible for a range of other diseases and conditions such as cancer, diabetes, tooth decay, and gout, and it is actually not at all nutritious for your body. Of course, as with many things in life, raw sugar in moderation is both healthy and desirable. However, with the high concentrations of refined sugars in so many of the products we consume daily, sometimes in unexpected places, eating sugar only in moderation is a big challenge. We all have a choice: accept the challenge, or accept the frightening consequences of eating too much sugar.

References

Choi, H. K., & Curhan, G. (2008). Soft drinks, fructose consumption, and the risk of gout in men: prospective cohort study. *The British Medical Journal*, 336 : 309 doi: 10.1136/bmj.39449.819271.BE

Diabetes UK (October 2009) Retrieved August 18, 2010 from http://www.diabetes.org.uk/ Guide-to-diabetes/Introduction-to-diabetes/What_is_diabetes/

Eberhardt, M. S., Ogden, C., Engelgau, M., Caldwell, B., Hedley, A. A., & Saydah, S. H. (2004). Prevalence of overweight and obesity among adults with diagnosed diabetes—United States, 1988-1994 and 1999-2002. *MMWR Morbidity and Mortality Weekly Report*, *53*(45): 1066-1068. PMID 15549021.

Gascoigne, B. (2001). History of the cultivation of plants. *HistoryWorld*. Retrieved October 1, 2010, from http://www.historyworld.net/wrldhis/plaintexthistories .net/wrldhis/plaintexthistories.asp?historyid=ab56

Haslam, D.W., & James, W.P.T. (2005). Obesity. *The Lancet*, *366*(9492), 1197-1209.

Kelley, A. E., & Berridge, K. C. (2002). The neuroscience of natural rewards: Relevance to addictive drugs. *The Journal of Neuroscience*, *22*(9), 3306-3311.

Kirschen, D. (2010, July 10). What are the benefits of removing refined sugar from one's diet? Livestrong.com database. Retrieved August 18, 2010, from http://www.livestrong.com/ article/189203-what-are-the-benefits-of-removing-refined-sugar-from-ones-diet/

Klisiewicz, R. (2010, February 3). The dangers of refined sugar and its impact on fitness. Ezine Articles database. Retrieved August 18, 2010, from http:// ezinearticles.com/?The-Dangers-of-Refined-Sugar-and-Its-Impact-on-Fitness&id=3683366

Norris, J. (2009, June 25). Sugar is a poison, says UCSF obesity expert. *Science Café*. Retrieved August 19, 2010, from http://www.ucsf.edu/science-cafe/ articles/obesity-and-metabolic-syndrome-driven-by-fructose-sugar-diet/

United States Department of Agriculture nutrient database. Retrieved August 18, 2010, from http://www.nal.usda.gov/fnic/foodcomp/cgi-bin/list_nut_edit.pl

Vecchia, C. L., Franceschi, S., Bidoli, E., Barbone, F. and Dolara, P. (1993), Refined-sugar intake and the risk of colorectal cancer in humans. *International Journal of Cancer, 55*, 386–389. DOI: 10.1002/ijc.2910 550308.

World Health Organization (2003, August 23). *Populations with high sugar consumption are at increased risk of chronic disease, South African researchers report* [Press Release]. Retrieved August 20, 2010, from http://www.who.int/bulletin/releases/2003/PR0803/en/

World Health Organization (2003, August 23). *Obesity*. Retrieved September 2, 2010, from http://www.who.int/topics/obesity/en/

The treatment of plagiarism

Below are authentic excerpts, taken from the respective websites, of how some universities officially deal with instances of plagiarism.

After each example, the numbers in brackets refer to which of the punishments below are explicitly referenced.

1. A warning from the professor	7. A monetary fine
2. Need to write the paper again	8. Suspension from the university
3. A formal apology	9. Expulsion from the university
4. Failure of the paper	10. Limited career opportunities
5. Failure of the course	11. A lawsuit
6. Failure of the degree	12. Prison

Oxford University, U.K. (6, 9)

Intentional or reckless plagiarism may incur severe penalties, including failure of your degree or expulsion from the university.

http://www.admin.ox.ac.uk/edc/goodpractice/about/

Harvard University, U.S. (9)

Students who, for whatever reason, submit work either not their own or without clear attribution to its sources will be subject to disciplinary action, and ordinarily required to withdraw from the College.

http://isites.harvard.edu/fs/docs/icb.topic25367.files/Plagiarism_Policy.htm

The Australian National University (1, 2, 3, 4, 5, 8)

If, after consideration of the matter, the prescribed authority finds that the student has engaged in misconduct[1], the prescribed authority may:

a. decide to take no action; or

b. order a re-assessment in a program or course to which the alleged misconduct is related (which may include, for example, requiring the student to re-sit an examination for a maximum pass grade of 50% or determining that an alternative form of examination be completed by the student); or

c. deny the student access to all or any of the facilities of the University or to all or any part of the University premises, or to any activities conducted by or on behalf of the University for a specified period not exceeding 12 months; or

d. reprimand the student; or

e. cancel, adjust, or award any passing grade for any examination, test or other assessment of the student's academic work or standing; or

[1] Misconduct includes plagiarism.

f. terminate the candidature or enrolment of the student in a program of study or course in which the student is admitted or enrolled and prohibit the resumption of candidature or enrolment for a period not exceeding 12 months; or

g. determine the conditions under which the student may attend classes or lessons or use any facility of the University; or

h. if the misconduct involved so warrants, refer the matter to the Vice-Chancellor; or

i. require the student to apologise or take other action the prescribed authority thinks appropriate with a view to mitigating the effect of the misconduct; or

j. take any action that is a combination of the actions referred to in paragraphs

http://www.anu.edu.au/cabs/rules/DisciplineRules.pdf

The Australian National University, College of Law (10)

A finding of academic misconduct may also jeopardise a student's admission to legal practice.

http://law.anu.edu.au/Undergraduate/PDFs%20for%20Undergrad%20Policy/Student_Academic_Integrity_2010.pdf

University of Cape Town, South Africa (4, 5, 9, 10)

By committing plagiarism you will get zero for the plagiarised work, and may fail the course. In addition, the matter must be referred to the Vice-Chancellor or nominee for possible disciplinary action in terms of the rules on disciplinary jurisdiction and procedures (DJP1.1) against you. If this is the case, and the plagiarism is substantial, the Registrar has indicated that, unless there are unusual circumstances, the prosecution will ask for your expulsion. Even if you are not expelled, a conviction for cheating on your academic record is likely to limit your career opportunities. If you are preparing for a profession, you should know that a conviction for cheating in academic work may bar you from professional licensing temporarily or permanently.

http://www.uct.ac.za/downloads/uct.ac.za/about/policies/plagiarism_students.pdf

Note: universities might be vague in their description. Oxford University, for example, talks of "severe penalties" but does not specify exactly what these might be. This means that a combination of some or many punishments could be possible.

Macmillan Education
4 Crinan Street
London N1 9XW
A division of Macmillan Publishers Limited
Companies and representatives throughout the world

ISBN 978-0-230-42194-3

Text © Dorothy E Zemach, Daniel Broudy,
Chris Valvona 2011

Design and illustration © copyright Macmillan Publishers
Limited 2011

Written by Dorothy E Zemach, Daniel Broudy,
Chris Valvona

First published 2011

Designed by xen
Illustrated by John Graham, Ciaran Hughes, Will Mitchell
and Vicky Woodgate
Cover design by xen based on a design by Jackie Hill at
320 Design
Cover illustration/photograph by xen
Picture research by Zoë Spilberg

Authors' acknowledgements
Dorothy Zemach:
Thank you to instructors at the American English Institute
at the University of Oregon who spoke with me and
allowed me to observe their research writing paper classes:
Tom Delaney, Elizabeth Root, Bonnie Tibbets, and Keli
Yerian. Thanks also to Bruce Rogers and Jaimie Scanlon
for their input on early drafts, to Carole Hughes for her
detailed attention to the later drafts, and to Adam Peneberg
for his discussion of the Stephen Glass case through
personal corresponadence. And as always, an undying
thanks to Will and Sebastian Mitchell for their love and
patience as I worked on this project.
Daniel Broudy:
Many thanks to my patient and understanding spouse,
Yuna, my daughter, Yena, and my enterprising students at
Okinawa Christian University whose inventive ideas about
conducting research led me to some new insights.
Chris Valvona:
I'm very grateful to my incredibly patient and supportive
wife, Ayano. Thanks also to the great students at Okinawa
Christian University for providing ideas and inspiration,
and many thanks to Aki Nakaema for being such a good
sounding board (without even knowing it).

The publishers would like to thank Liz Hunt and
Troy McConachy.

The authors and publishers would like to thank the
following for permission to reproduce their photographs:

Alamy pp8(tr, m), 18, 39(r), 50(tc), 85;

Corbis pp7, 8(tl), 23(l), 39(c),60, 67;

Getty pp8(br), 23(r), 39(l);

Macmillan Publishers LTD (with kind of consent of each
publisher) p50(tl, tcr, tr, bl, nc);

NASSA p100;

Photodisc p2;

Superstock pp5, 8(bl), 23(c), 49, 50(br), 51, 84.

Boost Media Solutions, LLC p101
Boost Media Solutions, LLC shall not be responsible or
liable, directly or indirectly, for any damage or loss caused
or alleged to be caused by or in connection with use of or
reliance on any such Content, goods or services available
on or through any such site or resource.
The authors and publishers are grateful for permission to
reprint the following copyright material:

Page 120: Material from webpages 'Discipline Rules 2007'
and 'Student Academic Integrity' copyright © Australian
National University 2011;
Page 48: Material reproduced from British Medical Journal,
H.K. Choi and Gary Curhan, Vol. 336 No. 7639, copyright ©
2008, with permission from BMJ Publishing Group Ltd.;
Page 63: Material from article 'The Use of Color as a
Tool for Propaganda' copyright © 2007, reprinted with
permission of the publisher;
Page 46: Material from article 'The Dangers of Refined
Sugar and its Impact on Fitness' copyright © 2011
reprinted with permission of the author;
Page 119: Material from webpage 'Plagiarism and
Collaboration' copyright © Harvard College 2011;
Page 47: Material from article 'Obesity' copyright ©
01.10.05 The Lancet, Volume 366, Issue 9492, pages 1197-
1209, reprinted with permission of Elsevier;
Page 46, 114: Material from article 'What are the benefits of
removing refined sugar from one's diet?' copyright ©
30.07.10 used with permission of the publisher;
Page 55: Material from article 'Prevalence of Overweight
and Obesity among Adults with Diagnosed Diabetes'
copyright © 2004 used with permission of the Morbidity
and Mortality Weekly Report;
Page 68: Material from 'Wings of Morning' copyright ©
1995 Thomas Childers. Reprinted by permission of Perseus
Books, a member of the Perseus Books Group;
Page 68: Material from 'THE WILD BLUE: THE MEN AND
BOYS WHO FLEW THE B-24S OVER GERMANY' by
Stephen Ambrose. Copyright © 2001 by Ambrose-Tubbs,
Inc. Reprinted with the permission of Simon & Schuster,
Inc.and Simon & Schuster UK. All Rights Reserved;
Page 55: Material from article 'Sugar is a poison, says
UCSF Obesity Expert' copyright © 25.06.09 used with
permission of the author;
Page 120: Material from webpage 'Avoiding Plagiarism:
A Guide for Students' copyright © 2011 reprinted with
permission of the University of Cape Town;
Page 119: Material from webpage 'Plagiarism' copyright
© 2011 reprinted with permission of the University of
Oxford;
Page 48, 115: Material from article 'Refined-sugar intake
and the risk of colorectal cancer in humans' copyright ©
30.09.93 reprinted with permission of the publisher;
Page 47, 115: Research information used from http://www.
who.int/bulletin/releases/2003/PR0803/en/ and http://
www.who.int/mediacentre/factsheets/fs311/en/index.html,
with kind permission of World Health Organisation;
Page 73: Material used from 'Science and Movies: My New
Essay in Nature' and 'Communication: learning to love
science films' copyright © 2010 reprinted with permission
of the author and Macmillan Publishers Ltd: Nature 468,
35-36;

These materials may contain links for third party websites.
We have no control over, and are not responsible for, the
contents of such third party websites, please use care when
accessing them.

Although we have tried to trace and contact copyright
holders before publication, in some cases this has not been
possible. If contacted we will be pleased to rectify any
errors or omissions at the earliest opportunity

Printed and bound in Thailand

2018 2017 2016
10 9 8 7 6 5